Do What Matters

ENDORSEMENTS FOR *DO WHAT MATTERS*

Teresa McCloy writes from a deep well of ministry and life experience. Her heart for people comes through loud and strong in these pages. She's a perfect companion for all those who want to learn how to truly rest in God.

–**Rory Noland**, Director of Heart of the Artist Ministries

In her inspiring book, *Do What Matters*, Coach, Speaker & Creator of, the REALIFE Process®, LLC, Teresa McCloy helps us learn to live from a place of rest rather than rush. For anyone currently living what Teresa calls a "hair-on-fire life," and wants to truly take control of their time and mindset, this is the perfect book for you. From discovering how to live your REALIFE to asking ourselves, "How do I want to live so I can be who I want to be?" *Do What Matters* is a powerful playbook to the reset we've been needing in order to live a more restful and intentional life.

–**Tommy Breedlove** - *Wall Street Journal* and *USA Today* Best Selling Author of the Book *Legendary.*

As a fellow speaker and author, Teresa McCloy has mastered her message that it's possible to move from living with your hair on fire to enjoying the ordinary moments that, in reality, are truly extraordinary. *Do What Matters* is more than "shelf" help. It's self-help that is practical and sustainable. From the stage to the page, Teresa is the REAL deal.

–**Kent Julian**, *CSP Professional Speaker*

Do What Matters is more than a book. It's a deeply spiritual, yet profoundly practical guide for living a life that matters. Read it. Enjoy it. Apply it, and then embody it. You and those you love will be glad you did.

–**Kim Avery**, MA, Certified Business Coach, Author of *The Prayer Powered Entrepreneur*

As a mom of three kids with an online business and a team, I struggled to compartmentalize life and work! Thankfully, Teresa McCloy says, 'It all belongs.' *Do What Matters* provides a remarkable, repeatable framework to align your whole life, embrace your values, and give time and energy toward what matters most, all while avoiding overwhelm.

–**Natalie Eckdahl**, Host of the BizChix Podcast, Author of *R.E.S.E.T Your Mindset,* CEO Biz Chix, Inc.

A truly important read. Teresa's powerful vulnerability as she shares her story and her tangible structures for progress naturally leads her readers to a more peaceful and present life. The world needs this book.

–**Justin Janowski** - Coach

BizableTV features everyday, ordinary entrepreneurs with stories of determination, perseverance, and success. Teresa McCloy's *Do What Matters–Live from Rest, Not Rush* is one of those extraordinary REALIFE stories. Her story will inspire you and better yet, provide a sustainable process to reclaim what you value most personally and professionally.

–**Paul Klein**, *Co-Founder of BizableTV*

What a blessing to have the teaching of Teresa McCloy in book form! God has gifted her with clear communication, humor, and the ability to see exactly the issues with which I struggle. The Realife Process® is exactly what I needed to make the important things important, connect to purpose, and put the adversity and trials of this world in context. This is a must-read for everyone seeking to make the next season of life their best yet regardless of what is in the past.

–**John Ramstead**, CEO of Beyond Influence and host of the Eternal Leadership podcast

Pure Gold! Through her book and the REALIFE Process®, Teresa McCloy invites us to remember what matters most and intentionally take action rather than participating in the exhausting grind of busyness. Relational repairs and healthy interactions take intention and attention. Applying her REALIFE insights to the rhythms of our daily lives with The Enneagram Harmony Model is a sacred combination that leads to whole life transformation! We have personally benefited from Teresa living what she believes in both work and relationships.

–**Rev. Clare and Rev. Scott Loughrige**, Lead Pastors Crossroads Church and Ministries, Authors *Motions of the Soul, The ©iEnneagram and Spiritual Rhythms for the Enneagram.*

It's not often you come across a book that leaves you this informed AND inspired. The next time I'm asked for advice on how to live a meaningful life, 'Read Teresa McCloy's book, *Do What Matters* will be the next words out of my mouth.

–**Mike Kim**, *Wall St. Journa*l bestselling author of *You Are the Brand*

It has been such a wonderful privilege to walk alongside Teresa in this last year as I began to see this book *Do What Matters* come to life. For the last few years, I have seen Teresa walk out the very words in this book well before anything was ever written on a page. In fact, watching her walk this journey of personal and professional growth continues to inspire me to truly pursue the things that really matter, to take time to slow down, to introduce purposeful rhythms in my own life and to start living more wholistically from my being and not just my doing. Becoming real is hard work but well worth the time and effort it takes to live a full circle life.

–**Victoria Mininger**, Founder & CEO Bear Creek Outdoor Living & Author of *"Daring To Fight – When Grit, Grace & Faith Take Depression Head On.*

DO WHAT MATTERS

Live from Rest Not Rush Using the REALIFE Process®

TERESA MCCLOY

NASHVILLE

NEW YORK • LONDON • MELBOURNE • VANCOUVER

DO WHAT MATTERS

Live From Rest, Not Rush, Using The REALIFE Process®

© 2023 Teresa McCloy

All rights reserved. No portion of this book may be reproduced, stored in a retrieval system, or transmitted in any form or by any means—electronic, mechanical, photocopy, recording, scanning, or other—except for brief quotations in critical reviews or articles, without the prior written permission of the publisher.

Published in New York, New York, by Mount Tabor Media, a branded imprint of Morgan James Publishing. Morgan James is a trademark of Morgan James, LLC.
www.MorganJamesPublishing.com

Proudly distributed by Ingram Publisher Services.

A **FREE** ebook edition is available for you or a friend with the purchase of this print book.

CLEARLY SIGN YOUR NAME ABOVE

Instructions to claim your free ebook edition:
1. Visit MorganJamesBOGO.com
2. Sign your name CLEARLY in the space above
3. Complete the form and submit a photo of this entire page
4. You or your friend can download the ebook to your preferred device

ISBN 9781631959066 paperback
ISBN 9781631959073 ebook
Library of Congress Control Number: 2022932912

Cover Design by:
Christopher Kirk
www.GFSstudio.com

Interior Design by:
Chris Treccani
www.3dogcreative.net

DEDICATION

To my family, who have walked this full-circle journey with me.

To my amazing and patient husband, Dale, who has always believed in me and our kids. You have supported me even when my hair was on fire.

To our daughter, Anneke, who is courageous and wise beyond her years. You've brought light into our lives from the first day we saw you halfway around the world—a beautiful blonde toddler full of love and joy. And to our son-in-law, Justin, who has been an added blessing to our lives in more ways than you will ever know.

To our son, Eric, who left this earth far too soon. We miss your humor and wit and the presence you brought to a room with your smile. Your life on this earth made an impact on your family and so many others. You have helped us be REAL!

TABLE OF CONTENTS

HOW TO READ THIS BOOK

As you read this book, you will be introduced to key concepts that use existing words in the English language that we have then, for the purposes of this book, defined how they fit into the REALIFE Process®.

As you read, you will see certain words such as *Rest*, *Needs*, *Values*, etc. italicized at first mention. In this instance, the italicized words are words I have defined for use around the REALIFE Process®. These key definitions can be easily found in the back of the book in the glossary of terms for ongoing reference as you read through the book.

It is key to note that while this book is intended to be read initially in order from chapter 1 through chapter 10, certain chapters—in particular chapters 3–7—can later be referenced individually as you begin to incorporate the key components of the REALIFE Process® into your life.

Enjoy the Process!

FOREWORD

Being

We have become his poetry, a re-created people that will fulfill the destiny he has given each of us, for we are joined to Jesus, the Anointed One. Even before we were born, God planned in advance our destiny and the good works we would do to fulfill it! Ephesians 2:10 TPT

When I first met Teresa, she was in the beginnings of "Doing What Matters" and strangely enough, it was not about doing. She was coming present to "being" so that she would be able to do what mattered. Over time that experience re-oriented her to doing the unique works that God has given her to do. She came to a place in life where she could no longer go the way she was going. As Teresa began to understand that truth it created an openness to journey into her more authentic self that would be a gift to others. If you are reading this, you are one of the "others."

At the time of our introduction to one another, Teresa had been meeting with a Spiritual Director who had then invited her to attend The Transforming Center. This two-year community experience, led by Ruth Haley Barton, was based on teaching that was came from Ruth's book *Sacred Rhythms*. During this time Teresa stepped into the rhythms of being that included, retreat, slowing, silence and solitude, a daily examen, discernment, loving your neighbor, listening to scripture as it spoke to her and learning to craft a rule of life that allowed her to practice living life, "doing what matters."

After a decade of serving as a Spiritual Mentor at The Transforming Center, Teresa and I began to meet on a regular basis so I could walk with her on her journey with God. Over the years the good work that God has given me to do is to listen to a person's story and help them uncover the presence of God in the whole of it, even the most difficult parts of a story.

Teresa's story began to unfold as we talked about the generations of farming that pepper her story and how, as a result, "doing" is planted into the soil of her life. As I listened to her story, "productivity" had taken top billing and the practices of Resting, Renewing, Reviewing, were not a part of this farming and "doing" lifestyle. As her life unfolded, with school, hobbies, work, and relationships — the "way of the farm" entered each of those places with consistent themes of not doing enough and the need to prove herself. This posture resulted in the needs of personal rest, refreshment, and review to go into hiding.

But then, Teresa began to taste the goodness of the Lord in a new way. His love and acceptance came before any doing. She allowed herself time, trusted relationships, listening, and then responding. As in the story of the Velveteen Rabbit, it requires time, presence and listening to hear, respond and receive that voice of love that comes from God.

Her adopted son Eric became one of the pathways of facing her own addiction to work and productivity. In a most tender way Eric's story reveals that God can use all things for good for those called according to His purposes.

As we continued to meet, Teresa decided to enter a two-year Certification in Spiritual Direction with Sustainable Faith at The

Springs — a retreat center where my husband and I are co-directors. I teach the course, so our relationship deepened. Teresa found herself back in a farm type setting receiving back some of what was missed in earlier years. Her responsibility was to simply be, to listen, to learn, to be in community and to engage the land, but not for its productivity, but for its goodness, beauty, and truth. She spent time sitting on a bench, walking the trails and the labyrinth, slowing, sitting around a dinner table, being read to, practicing being listened to, and listening to another.

That is now the kind of space she is creating at her home and their family farm where she, and now others, can come and retreat. We each hold a beauty that is to be a gift in the world, in the time that we live on the earth. The outflow of what Teresa has learned is not just for herself, but now for the sake of others as well.

Do What Matters calls forth the invitation to facing yourself as is, of engaging with community, of slowing and entering practices that open one to the presence of God.

Two questions we must answer for ourselves is: Who do I want to be? and, How do I want to live? Taking responsibility for those questions becomes a journey into "real reality" and to the "real you."

This first invitation is to hear and receive that you are a beloved daughter or son of the most high God. To realize that His favor is on you, you are beloved, and that he is glad that you are on the earth at this time. This invitation sets you on a journey of letting go of the ways that the world tries to define for all of us.

What Teresa has outlined in this book is a structure and a process called "The REALIFE Process®" that creates a greater freedom to live the life that you have been created to live. It is a process that has important personal work — naming our needs and values, creating areas of focus, naming projects to work on, creating blocks of time to be with God in an ordinary day, being present to self-care, being present to others, and to prepare for the work of the day seeing that each ordinary day carries extraordinary sightings.

This book is an invitation to become a part of the REALIFE Process® community. It is a place to grow and learn personally and become together what we cannot do well on our own.

Entering the REALIFE Process® truly has the possibility of reorienting your life to *doing what matters* with the one and only life you have.

Pay Attention.
Be Astonished.
Tell About it.
By Mary Oliver

Sybil Towner – Spiritual Director and co-author of *Listen to my Life* and co-founder of *One Life Maps.*

FOREWORD

Doing

I've always loved setting big goals at the beginning of each year. In fact, I am consistent about having my goals completed for the coming year, in seven different areas of my life, by November 14th of each preceding year. Thus, I have them clarified, planted in my mind, and typically see major progress even in those 48 remaining days of the year.

But recently I've been challenged by some people I love and trust about the necessity of approaching the new year in that manner. People whom I highly admire, who are kind and loving, and also very high achievers. In digging into deep conversations I've discovered that often they are living more from a Rule of Life than from a rigid, structured to-do list that seems to bear resemblance to my annual process.

It's been said that we achieve inner peace when our schedule and financial records are aligned with our values. And it appears that a Rule of Life is a wonderful method for establishing that harmony. In this book, you'll read that a Rule of Life is answering two questions: Who do I want to be? And, how do I want to live?

And I find there's a long history for this concept. While admitting the Old Testament, in general, conjures up more confusion than enlightenment for me I still occasionally find a morsel that causes me to dig deeper. In Judges 13, we find the story of Samson's mother and father being told about his upcoming birth. An angel had appeared to Samson's mother. He gave her detailed instructions about becoming pregnant and giving birth to this son who was going to be a special leader for the children of Israel.

Manoah, the Daddy-to-be wanted to check this guy out — not knowing it was really an angel. So he asked to see him as well and when they met he had one important question: "Now let Your words come to pass! What will be the boy's rule of life, and his work?" Judges 13:12 (NKJV)

There is that concept again - being asked even before a child is born. And serving as a reminder to each of us. What are the principles and values that lead our daily actions? How do those daily actions define and blend into the work we do - that create the person we become?

There's something worth pondering. Have you asked that about your own children? Do you ask that daily for yourself?

These two things — one's rule of life (what we could call one's principles or values and daily actions that are expressed by those principles and values) together with the work one believes he or she has been given to do — create the person we become.

In this book you are about to read, Teresa gently walks us through a process for thoughtfully deciding how we want to order and align our days in a way that will bring us life instead of chaos. How to take the muddy water we're often trying to make sense of and see it settle into a rhythm that is clear and life-giving.

So I can look at my top ten Values - Abundance, Creativity, Gratitude, Beauty, Vision, Integrity, Continuous Improvement, Inner Harmony, Change & Variety, Success. Am I living those out daily? And then look at my work. Do I have a clear sense that this is more significant than just a way to generate income?

When we know what we are called to do, are clear on our values and principles, and are developing the daily habits to blend those, then we can be confident our life has meaning and purpose.

So here's the question: "what shall be the rule of your life and your work?" If you can solve that question, today and every day, your life will not be pointless but will be meaningful, purposeful, and profitable.

I'm honored to recommend this journey where Teresa guides us into her "REALIFE Process®" where we can, like the Velveteen Rabbit, become real in the truest sense of the word.

Dan Miller *New York Times* bestselling, author of
48 Days to the Work You Love

INTRODUCTION

I don't remember turning 50. I know that I did considering the fact that, as I sit and write this, I am now in my 60th year of life. And yet the details of that birthday join the other shadowy dates and times that were a blur of the life I lived 10 years ago.

Back then, I was deep in my career as a full-time minister, on staff at a small but growing church in our tiny rural community. My life revolved around that growing church and my growing ministry career. It was all we talked about and focused on. I lived and breathed church. It was all I knew. And as the church strived for continued growth and I strived for continued affirmation I found myself leaning into the work and busyness of it all. That was the kind of pace that fed my personality and addiction and need for success and high performance. Yet, right alongside that need for success and performance lived an undeniable fear of failure and a life teetering on the brink of disaster.

Because I worked at such a fast pace, I never noticed the disaster ahead of me. That pace and my drive for success helped me push past any warning signs. There was work to get done, kids to raise, and a husband to lend my support to. I was too busy living with my hair on fire to notice that our family was heading for a landmine.

Who had time to figure that out? I barely had enough time to look past the surface-level issues of my work, helping my daughter navigate her junior high school years, and trying to help my 24-year-old son who seemed to be fighting his own battles, though we couldn't quite put a finger on exactly what those were.

So there I was, striving to succeed in my career, working to pastor the families in our church, and trying to be the best mom on the planet—available to attend every game and counsel every challenge that can greet a junior high girl and young adult son. And did I mention the fact that I was also married to a full-time farmer? A farmer and husband who also carried the weight of the world on his shoulders as he worked to support our family. Day in and day out, he worked the land on our fourth-generation family farm with his own father and our son, all the while trying to carry his and my stress alike. In those days, we focused on three things: farming, church, and our kids, juggling all those things on hyperdrive for so long that, over time, hyperdrive became normal to us. Internally, my own emotional, physical, spiritual, and relational health was suffering, and I had this uneasy feeling that at some point something was going to have to give. I just hoped that when it did, I could manage the damage once the smoke had settled.

Have you ever had those moments in life where you just know you're about to step on a landmine? Yet the thing about landmines is that you don't usually see them until it's too late. Deep in my gut, I knew we were in dangerous territory, living the pace of life we were living. Our life was its own minefield with one crisis after another, at church and at home. In particular was the baffling behavior of our son.

Dale and I spent many a late night having long conversations, trying to figure out what was really going on with Eric. Divinely, over the past several months, I had begun to recognize the chaos my life was in. The 80-hour work weeks, the time spent away from home attending church meetings and events, and the stress that was present in all of our lives were beginning to catch up to me.

We were becoming very much aware that our beautiful 24-year-old son, Eric, the one who stood over six feet tall and always brought a presence into the room, was very much struggling to find his way. However, it wasn't until the bomb went off in our home that we would grasp just how much he was struggling. The day was September 23, 2011, just two months past my 50th birthday. Maybe that's why I can't remember that birthday: because from the moment Eric sat down at the kitchen table and opened his mouth to share his pain, I knew our lives would never be the same.

The Bomb

That fall morning was beautiful with the trees outside having changed to what seemed like 12 different shades of color. As a farming family, we were at the height of fall harvesting. With all that harvest can entail, I had asked the church leaders if I could work from home one day a week so I could be more present with my family. The church was over 20 miles away, and it was easy to spend hours traveling the blacktop from our farm to the church and additional school activities. The change of pace was nice, and I looked forward to not running so fast, at least for one day a week. Earlier I had driven our daughter to school and was back home brewing a fresh pot of coffee. I distinctly remember setting up my laptop at the kitchen table and settling in to get a little work done. I felt good about this healthier step toward being more present with my family.

Just as I started into my work for the day, our son, Eric, who had moved back home to help his dad with harvest, walked in the kitchen door and sat down across from me at the table. "Mom,

I need to talk to you." At that moment I wished I could just say, "Whatever it is, we can talk about it later; you're late and you need to go help your dad." But as Eric sat there, building the courage to speak, I could only sit silent and wait as this man/child, this precious boy that we had adopted at only five months old, was about to shed light on all of the questions and concerns we had been feeling about him for quite some time.

You know those moments in life that seem to shift into slow motion and the music builds like in a really bad movie? This was that moment for me. As I braced for his words, I knew this was the time for listening and nothing more. With tears gathering in the corners of his eyes, finding their way down his handsome face, and with a trembling voice and his whole body shaking, he simply said, "Mom, I'm addicted to heroin. I'm scared to death, and I don't know what to do."

Of all the things Eric could have told us, this is not what we were expecting. We knew he was drinking some and going through a scary amount of money, which he attributed to gambling. We knew he was struggling emotionally, physically, and spiritually. But drug addiction? And heroin?! How? When? Where? We had asked many times about drugs, and just as many times he had denied it. And we believed him. We believed him because he was our son and we loved him more than life itself.

That day would begin a very dark and painful six-year battle filled with events, stories, trauma, and heartache. A battle I wouldn't wish on any family. A battle that would fling shrapnel on anyone and everyone who was close and leave our family walking wounded for a very long time. And in my then typical fashion, not knowing how to yet live any differently, I decided I needed to DO something, anything, to fix this and get us back to normal as fast as possible. I was positive I could work my way through this but, first, I just had to get through the day.

After promising Eric that I would get him the help he needed, I sent him out the door to help his dad with the harvest. My brain needed time to process what had just happened. I had always been my son's biggest advocate through his years of school as he faced ADHD, making sure he graduated from high school and at least tried college. Dale had taught him how to farm, and Eric was a good farmer, taking naturally to the hard work and demands of the farm. He proudly worked beside his dad and grandpa. Yes! I could fix this and gain back the control that had been temporarily lost with Eric's life-shattering declaration.

And like a shell-shocked survivor, I scrambled to pick up the pieces of our shattered family, making calls, seeking out resources, and struggling to make sense of a world that we had never planned on visiting.

Less than 24 hours later, we were driving our 24-year-old son to the first of many, many treatment centers.

LIVING FROM RUSH

CHAPTER 1

A Hair-On-Fire Life

"He longed to become Real, to know what it felt like; and yet the idea of growing shabby and losing his eyes and whiskers was rather sad. He wished that he could become it without these uncomfortable things happening to him."

—Margery Williams, *The Velveteen Rabbit*

We had only been married a year when we found out we wouldn't be able to have our own biological children. I was 22 and Dale was 24. As I reflect on those early years and this first major hurdle in our young married lives, I can see my addictive and success-driven personality showing up as I worked to grasp this new reality.

Dale and I had met just two years earlier through a mutual friend. We dated for six months, got engaged, and got married just 14 months after our first date. During that year of dating, Dale worked hard to build us our first home on the family farm. We both looked forward to our wedding and this joyous and exciting time of life. Up until then, life had seemed on track until the day we found out that infertility would be a part of our marriage journey. It was the first time that "the wheels came off the wagon" as I jokingly say around the farm.

It took a year of testing after we got married to confirm we wouldn't be able to have our own biological children. As devastating as the news was, my doing and success-driven personality immediately kicked into full-blown performer mode, and I began looking for ways to fix what seemed to be broken. Looking back, I now see so clearly the unhealthy pattern by which I lived my life; never quite letting myself feel the grief and loss that visited my life but instead always pushing to find a way to spin it into success. I had approached loss and grief in childhood the same way, and the pattern had carried into my adult life. My default had become to attack grief and loss like any other challenge: taking charge, getting things done, and becoming an expert in that particular situation. This time wasn't any different.

"It's no big deal," I told Dale. "My aunt and uncle couldn't have children and adopted. We can too!" And in true hair-on-fire fashion, I dove headlong into the adoption journey, and in less than four years, we had adopted our son, Eric, at five months of age. Back in the early 1980s, adoption was a totally different experience than it is today. Back then, because we hadn't been married very long, we had to jump over hurdle after hurdle, but I was determined to make it happen no matter what. And I did!

Fast forward to 10 years later. I had just experienced a huge loss in my life from a failed business but, true to form, threw myself into overdrive, ignoring the grief and loss I should have worked through after my business failure, and, instead, began to pursue an adoption of a little girl from Romania. Our daughter was only 26 months old when she came to us and quickly became the joy of our lives. We all adored her. It had taken 14 months to cross all the hurdles that come with foreign adoption and yet, before we knew it, Dale, Eric, and I boarded a plane bound for Romania to bring little Anneke Bea Lynne home.

Hyperdrive Living

Eric was in sixth grade at the time, and getting a baby sister became the highlight of his young life. Having been diagnosed with ADHD, Eric found school extremely difficult. We spent many nights in long fights over homework and his struggle with it all. But, from the moment she stepped foot into our home, Anneke brought a light with her that brightened up the house. In some ways, it felt like a fresh new beginning for all of us. To Eric, Anneke became the joy of his life and he loved her to pieces. Anneke's arrival seemed to signal that life was good again and made us feel like our family was finally complete.

Despite the fullness of my days with now two children and a farmer husband to keep up with, I found myself always seeking something else to do. "Doing" came naturally to me, and I was always looking for what to dive into next. Shortly after getting married, I graduated with an associate degree in computer programming. Back then it was 1982 and we were still using floppy disks and punch cards. The thought of owning a computer you could carry around with you was laughable because, back then, computers were as big as an entire room. But even then technology moved fast, so my degree in computers became quickly outdated, even though my love for technology has never waned. Unfortunately, in rural southern Illinois, there wasn't much need for computer programmers, so I turned my attention away from computers to something else I loved: music.

Music had always been my way to express myself creatively and quickly became a performance platform for me when I shifted away from computer programming. It was a way to escape, express my emotions, and get the attention and affirmation I had craved ever since I was a small child. As a child, music was my escape into my own world, but I also used music to receive validation from others. (As I got older, I used music and a drive for success to achieve that same objective.) My greatest memory was the gift my parents gave to me the Christmas of my fourth grade year. It was an autoharp just like the one used by my music teacher at school. I loved it. With the autoharp, I could write my own music simply by pressing a bar that would create an exact chord. It was a life-changing gift for a 10-year-old child with music in her head and heart. It was a gift that opened a whole new world to me as I explored the language of writing songs and music. Even to this day, writing music and playing the piano are two of the most refreshing and relaxing things I do.

As I moved into my early 40s, my unhealthy behavior of seeking accomplishment and validation to prove that I was "enough" really began to be magnified. It started simply enough but soon morphed into filling my schedule with all kinds of commitments. It seemed that I had an inability to say no to anything because I said yes to everything people asked me to do. I felt like my entire life revolved around commitments to other people. I had no life rhythm or routines of my own.

By the time we were able to settle into a bit of a rhythm again, Anneke was a preschooler. I was teaching private school two days a week, operating a music studio from our home with 60 students, and volunteering and running the music and kids' programming at our small growing church. I was living with my hair on fire, but at least our life had some bit of a rhythm. I was happy, or so I thought.

Looking back, I can now see that those achievements and the fast pace of life I had created gave me an adrenaline rush that became my go-to addiction of choice. I felt a sense of euphoria from doing, achieving, and having people thank or compliment me for everything I did. It didn't help that I was good at all the things I did. Had I not been so good at some of them, I likely wouldn't have done so much because it was the success that fueled me rather than the busyness itself. But my ability to succeed in so many different areas at the same time kept me running on that crazy hamster wheel I called "life" at the time.

Five short years later, however, I started to feel my foundation crack a little. I began to feel and battle a range of emotions that I had been able to avoid over the years by filling my days with obligation after obligation. The same script kept running through my head: "How do I get out of this circus I am in? Will I ever be enough? Am I a good parent? Am I a good wife? Am I a good Christian? I am good, right?"

Round and round the thoughts went until the crazy tape I played in my head responded with "No, You're not enough. Better go find something better to do." And, just like that, I would flip my life upside down once again and start something new, often in a completely different direction.

BE PRESENT

CHAPTER 2

A REALIFE Coming Together

"Of what use was it to be loved and lose one's beauty and become Real if it all ended like this? And a tear, a real tear, trickled down his little shabby velvet nose and fell to the ground."

—Margery Williams, *The Velveteen Rabbit*

In the fall of 2006, I made a huge decision to take on a full-time ministry position as the creative arts minister at a church about 20 miles away from our farm. For a few years, I had been piecing together all kinds of jobs—teaching piano and voice in my own home music studio, teaching music at a nearby parochial school, and working at our local church part-time. Each job fueled my desire to succeed and be known for something, and yet, no matter how many jobs I worked, it never felt like I was doing enough. I thought that moving to one full-time job might be a stabilizing move for our family. And the creative arts minister role seemed like the perfect opportunity to bring all my gifts together in music, technology, organization, and teaching. I was certain my calling was to be in ministry and, truthfully, I loved it all.

For a number of years, it seemed like life couldn't get any better. We had great friends in our life, we were growing spiritually, and we were helping to lead a church. Yet I still couldn't escape that same feeling I had experienced while working multiple part-time jobs and overscheduling my life. There was something stirring beneath the surface, leaving me continually unsettled.

Much of my unsettledness seemed to revolve around our then nineteen-year-old son, Eric, and whether I was doing enough as his mother to support him. Eric, while funny and smart, could also be equally difficult, rebellious, and defiant. As he moved into high school, he and I had regular heated discussions about anything and everything, while Dale and Anneke frequently got caught in the crossfire of our debates. It was a stressful way to live but, over time, it became "normal" to all of us.

"Our yesterdays hold broken and irreversible things for us. It is true that we have lost opportunities that will never return, but God can transform this destructive anxiety into a constructive thoughtfulness for the future. Let the past rest, but let it rest in the sweet embrace of Christ. Leave the broken, irreversible past in His hands, and step out into the invincible future with Him."

—Oswald Chambers, *My Utmost for His Highest*

Holding on for Dear Life

Although I no longer worked three jobs, it didn't take long for me to work as if I still did, even in the one position as creative arts minister, a position I kept for over a decade. Pretty quickly after accepting the position, my workaholic tendencies rose to the surface once again. Working for the kingdom of God became my way to stop the crazy tape that always played in my head telling me, "You are not enough." Work, in my new full-time position, also became my escape from all that was going on at home that I could not control, most notably with Eric. The overworking and diving deeper into workaholic behavior did not happen overnight. It was a slow burn of taking on more and more responsibility and commitment at the church. It felt fun and exciting to be needed again.

On the surface I became a great leader, was an effective teacher, and had amazing friends. But the inner truth was that I was growing further and further away from God, my kids, and my husband. It wasn't just one thing that moved me further away from God either. A combination of the distance to work, helping our daughter through the anxiety of junior high, and the growing stress of a 20-year-old son who was slowly losing his way all blended together to fuel my workaholic behavior. That was how I coped. I dove into my work. And it didn't help that I was the only woman on staff in a full-time ministry position in our southern Illinois church community. I had so much to prove, didn't I? At least I thought I did.

Reflecting on those years, I see now that my doing and self-driven personality saw juggling all of those issues as a challenge. It fed my competitive nature to prove that I could succeed in a man's world all the while raising a wonderful family and being an amazing wife. I could bring home the bacon and fry it up, as they say. But at what cost? What was I really seeking? What was I really avoiding? What was the longing that seemed to rest deep within my soul? With all the busyness, I found it increasingly difficult to find my way anymore.

On the surface I became a great leader, was an effective teacher, and had amazing friends. But the inner truth was that I was growing further and further away from God, my kids, and my husband.

In all honesty, many of the days that made up the next four years were a blur for me. Deep inside, I felt like I was living life for everyone else. I desperately wanted to search for myself, and yet I hesitated, thinking that I had to hold everything together for others and didn't have room to do anything for myself. I wasn't the only one trying to find my way during those long and difficult years either.

Our son, by that point, was 25 years old and very much struggling with his addiction. Our daughter was also struggling, in her case, to figure out her own family identity. As Anneke moved into the high school years, she became increasingly curious about her own story and biological family. In an amazing twist of circumstances, she, through connections on Facebook, was able to locate her Romanian siblings half a world away. She began talking to them and dreamed of going to Romania to meet them for the very first time in person. In the midst of Anneke finding her siblings, Eric entered his first of many treatment centers in the fall of 2011.

A year later, in the summer of 2012, Anneke, a dear friend of mine, and I were finally able to visit Anneke's family in Romania. Like many parts of my life during that time, with the progress came pain. First, because we were traveling in the summer, Dale wasn't able to go with us to Romania. But even more challenging was that Eric had been admitted to his second treatment program in Minnesota that spring, and we flew to Romania a few months later. By that point, Eric had been struggling for quite some time to get a foothold and beat the addiction that had taken over his life.

Looking back, it is one of my biggest regrets not having Dale there beside us as we met Anneke's family. I wish we could have made it work. However, with Eric in treatment and not able to work on the farm, Dale was already overwhelmed with all the extra work that summer brings to the farm. Yet despite the stress at home, our time in Romania couldn't have been more wonderful. It was like a story out of a Hallmark movie. Every detail came together as we met not only our daughter's biological siblings but also her birth mother and entire birth family, including aunts, uncles, and even her grandmother. It was emotionally exhausting for all of us, especially for our 15-year-old daughter, yet there was joy in being reunited with this part of our daughter's world and her family.

As we experienced the rush of meeting Anneke's family, half a world away Eric was struggling in a halfway recovery house thousands of miles from home. He would eventually be kicked out of that place for relapsing once again, leading to long nights filled with conversations with Dale, Eric, and Eric's fiancé at the time. As I was halfway around the world, I was holding space in my heart and mind for both my son and daughter, and it was exhausting. Living in that reality was so very hard.

Upon returning from Romania, we decided to move Eric, his fiancé, and her two small children into a tiny house we had built for Eric on the farm just two years earlier. Building Eric a house on the farm had been our way of making an effort to manage his life before it got too far out of control. It truly seemed to be the best solution and the only way I knew how to not lose my entire family and myself in the process. Most days I fueled myself on coffee and adrenaline, navigating each crisis at home and work as they came.

And yet, as the next five years passed, Eric's addiction only worsened. Even with him so close to home, there was nothing we could do to stop it. We had no idea that God was still actively working behind the scenes.

Discovering a REALIFE

Despite all my planning and all my hard work, the course of my life would be impacted more by a decision I thought was inconsequential at the time than any of the other planned decisions I made that I thought would make a big impact.

Specifically, in 2011, I made the decision to invest in some mentor coaching to help me in my leadership as a creative arts minister. While it did help me become a more effective leader, it also led me to my own deep discoveries spiritually, mentally, emotionally, and physically. It led me to meeting Rory Noland, a gifted worship leader, mentor, and spiritual director. It would be Rory who would challenge me to begin the hard work of deep personal spiritual growth as I had never experienced before. In fact, in one particular session, he challenged me to sit quietly for five minutes a day from then until our next monthly session. When he challenged me, my initial reaction was, "You want me to do what?!" I couldn't imagine sitting still for one minute, and he wanted me to do five minutes straight?! Rory obviously saw in me what it would take me years to realize: that I was addicted to doing and using activity as a coping behavior.

Doing was my fix of choice when life was spinning out of control. It was the best way I knew to make it look like I was handling everything just fine while inside I was living like my hair was on fire. I will always be grateful that Rory took me by the hand and helped me begin the long journey toward living my REALIFE.

The parallel journey between my own recovery from my hair-on-fire lifestyle and my son's addiction was about to begin. And it was going to be a long hard road for both of us.

More than anything, I wish I could end this part of my story by saying that we all got better and that our family healed and rode off into the sunset. I wish I could say that we lived happily ever after. However, that was not the plan that God had for our family.

From that fall morning when Eric sat at our dining room table and revealed his addiction to me to the moment he passed away from a drug overdose on August 24, 2017, we lived every day on the edge of fear. In those seven years with Eric, we experienced multiple treatment centers, multiple arrests and felony charges, and long periods in jail. We spent months not knowing where Eric was, as he became homeless and lived on the streets. We watched him destroy not only his own life but others' lives as well, as he left a wake of destruction on many people he touched. We walked periods of recovery with him that became beautiful times together, and we saw him accept Christ as his Savior at a treatment program in 2014. But the fear of every family, that they will still lose the one they love, was finally brought to reality the day Eric lost his battle with the disease of addiction.

Obviously, there are so many details of our story that I haven't shared here, but really the details don't matter so much to this story. What does matter is the life of our son, Eric, and the work we all began to do, including him, to discover our REALSELF during those difficult years. Through Eric's life and his struggle with addiction, God showed me how to do the inner work to finally become real, and He did so in a very simple but profound way through the classic children's story of the Velveteen Rabbit. If you haven't ever read this poignant and powerful story by Margery Williams, I encourage you to look it up at your local library or even purchase your own copy. For me, one of the most powerful parts of the story is found midway through the book when the Skin Horse is explaining to the Velveteen Rabbit what it takes to become real: "When a child loves you for a long, long time, not just to play with, but REALLY love you, then you become Real." The Skin Horse wisely goes on to say, "once you are Real you can't become unreal again."

Now it was my turn to become real by doing the work of naming my adaptive coping behavior of workaholism and addressing my fear of failure and my need to succeed. It was time to learn how to talk openly about real things and not avoid hard conversations. Learn how to question my faith in a healthy way that would cause me to dig deeper. Learn to speak authentically about my feelings and thoughts. Own my actions and set good boundaries. Learn to pause and be fully present in the ordinary but extraordinary moments that happen each and every day. Learn to savor all these things as gifts from a loving, caring, and tender God.

They say the parent is the teacher, yet in my case, my children have been the true teachers. Helping to mold me by their own courageous struggles and victories. Challenging me to grow through their own unique stories. Through them, I have truly been given the gift of learning to live my own REALIFE.

Now it's your turn to join me in discovering your own REALIFE story.

BE REAL

CHAPTER 3

Crafting a *Modern Day Rule of Life*™

"You become. It takes a long time. That's why it doesn't happen often to people who break easily, or have sharp edges, or who have to be carefully kept. Generally, by the time you are Real, most of your hair has been loved off, and your eyes drop out and you get loose in the joints and very shabby. But these things don't matter at all, because once you are Real you can't be ugly, except to people who don't understand."

—Margery Williams, *The Velveteen Rabbit*

In the spring of 2011, when I started working with Rory Noland, I had ultimately decided to hire him because I knew that I could not sustain the pace I was currently running. I remember one morning, I snuck away into the nursing mothers' room at our church for a session with Rory. We always meet over the phone for my coaching session, and it was the one place in the building no one could find me. It had been a very hard week as it was Easter season and we were deep into planning weekend services at church. The pace was a hair-on-fire kind of pace at the church and wasn't much better at home. At home Eric was out of control and calling me several times a day for money or not showing up to work on the farm with his dad or simply needing me to "do" something for him. With our daughter, Anneke, in school almost 20 miles away, it also meant I was driving multiple trips back and forth to school and work to get her to all her practices and events.

My initial work with Rory had been intended to only relate to the ministry role I carried at the church. However, Eric's continued struggle with addiction, his stints in and out of jail, and Anneke herself being in some hard places meant that most days it was all I could do just to hold it together.

As I continued to work with Rory during this high-stress season, we started to focus on my own personal journey and not as much on my growth as a pastor that I had initially come to him for. It was somewhere during these initial meetings that Rory challenged me to sit quietly for the first time. There I was in the nursing mothers' room of our church, trying once again to do the right thing. I remember asking Rory several times, "What do you want me to do?"

In all honesty, I had never found something so hard to do in my entire life. For a woman who had lived her life only as it related to her doing, I struggled to just sit and be. Surely there was a way to do this right? So I just kept asking, "What was I supposed to think while I was sitting still? What was I supposed to feel? How would I know when I was done?" And yet despite all my questions and my struggle to really understand stillness, Rory was always so patient with me.

Almost from the first time I met Rory, I knew there was something different about him. He is a small and unassuming man, but he carries something peaceful in his inner being. A peace I desperately needed and was seeking in my own life.

After about two years of coaching, Rory invited me to become a part of a community of people at the Transforming Center, located in Chicago, Illinois, and led by Ruth Haley Barton. It was a God-led introduction because the transformational work I would do with this group would be pivotal in helping me learn to create a different way of doing life. A life that I was desperate for after so many years of running around with my hair on fire.

In the years working with Rory and then my time spent with the inspiring community at the Transforming Center, I realized how addicted I had become to the coping behavior of "doing." It was my fix of choice and the hit I needed when things were out of control as they often were in those days. On the outside, it looked like I was handling it all really well because my personality type is great at presenting that I have it all together and under control. However, the truth was, on the inside my life was completely out of control and a whirlwind of chaos, and it was taking its toll.

Fast forward to the spring of 2015 where, after almost 10 years of serving, I made the decision to step down from my pastoral role at the church. It was time. Stepping down meant so many things, but ultimately it meant I could be more present with Dale on the farm, in particular now that we had asked Eric to leave the farm for good. His addiction and behavior were a constant stress on Dale and our family that made those years of working and living together difficult. It was not an easy decision, and in some essence, it was the death of a long-held dream—of one day passing our farm to our son, Eric, so that he could continue the legacy of yet another generation working the soil. The decision was difficult for me, but for Dale, it was a loss beyond his imagination, and yet for the health of us all, we knew it was a necessary move. Coming home would also allow me to be more available to our daughter, who was entering her senior year of high school.

Despite all the turmoil that was happening within our family, God continued to heal me in so many ways during those years. Through the blessing of the community at the Transforming Center and beginning to meet with a spiritual director and a coach, I was learning to set boundaries and to open up to others and allow them to love me. I was learning to be authentic about my life and our story as a family. And as only God can, He continued to bring relationships into our lives that became so life-giving and supportive during those difficult years. The gift of deep friendships that formed with people during those years is a gift I hold sacred. For once, I was ready to let others love me with the love of Christ and stop striving to do it all on my own anymore. When I look back, I now see Christ surrounding me with a circle of connections, community, and the love that would eventually carry me through some of my darkest days to come.

During those years I discovered spiritual practices and rhythms that would begin to reshape my life and bring stability to the chaos. Four times a year, I would participate in quarterly retreats at the Transforming Center and found it to be the safe community and space I needed for my soul. Those retreats lead me to learn more about specific spiritual practices such as silence and solitude, prayer, discernment, honoring my body, and engaging with scripture in new ways. It was in this community that I was first introduced to working with a spiritual director by the name of Sibyl Towner and the Enneagram personality tool. These practices and tools became transformational in helping me discover and examine my life in ways I had never known before. My eyes were wide open to this new way of just being in the world with God instead of narrowly focusing on doing, fixing, and controlling my life.

During my time with the Transforming Center, I also met Ruth Haley Barton, author of *Sacred Rhythms*, as well as the founder of the Transforming Center. During one of our first sessions together, Ruth shared with us a powerful illustration of the difference between a chaotic life and one lived in peace. She recounted her own work with her spiritual director who said to her one day: You are like a jar of river water all shaken up. What you need is to sit still long enough that the sediment can settle, and the water can become clear.

As Ruth shared that story, I was struck by the visual of that small jar of river water. That was my life exactly. All shaken up with no clarity whatsoever. If I wanted to gain clarity, it was going to be vital that I learn to be still and allow things to settle. Following that weekend, I went down to the creek not far from our home, toting along a mason jar, dipping it deeply into the stream to gather my own river water.

I carried it home that day and placed it in my office. Today, these many years later, it continues to sit in my office, reminding me that I have to come from a place of "being" first before the "doing." If I come to life with doing first, life quickly becomes very clouded and unclear. Instead I have the choice to daily, weekly, and monthly settle myself into rhythms, routines, and patterns that honor who God created me to be. A life lived with clarity and not chaos.

In the following years, as I have developed my own process for living life from rest, not rush, I have begun to share that process with others. It truly has been a privilege to see others also use the process in the work they are doing. Over the years, the REALIFE Process® has become a set of tools that guide people to create a new way to approach and live their life, guided by their own new *Modern Day Rule of Life™*.

I have also had the privilege of walking with individuals who are learning to lean into the process of becoming real, of learning to sit still and operate out of their being and not their doing.

Today we are also blessed to train and certify facilitators around the country to work with these tools. One such person, and now close friend, is Winston Faircloth, one of our *REALIFE Process® Certified Facilitators*. In a sit-down conversation, he shared with me that "the process helped me clarify what is most important in my life. Now as I live more congruently with those needs and values I identified through the REALIFE Process, I find that I am a lot less stressed, anxious, and fearful. In fact, I feel like I'm becoming real again, not unlike the Velveteen Rabbit, realizing that I am not my circumstances and I'm not my achievements. I want to live my WHOLE life, not just my work anymore!"

REALIFE in REAL LIFE

The REALIFE Process gave me, personally, a structure that created freedom.

When I say structure, I mean rhythms, boundaries, and systems. This structure created support that I needed to thrive and feel free. I realized that fun was something I valued and was an important part of my Areas of Focus. I created a local bucket list that included things like a hot air balloon festival, sunflower fields, pickleball, and kayaking.

It also allowed scheduled time to have some alone time. My "me" time would always get pushed back because of things that came up with kids and work. Scheduling time has helped ensure I get time for solitude and reflection. The REALIFE Process has given me words to my purpose and helped me be clear with what is important and where I want to go. Understanding who I am at my core has allowed me to live how I want to live so I can then do my best work.

—Janna Thomason, REALIFE Process Certified Facilitator

A Rule of Life

It was during my time with the Transforming Center that I first learned about the concept of creating a personal rule of life. If you are not familiar with the practice of a rule of life, let me share some of the background with you. In AD 516, Saint Benedict developed a rule of life to help monks bring simple order to their days. The rule of life centered around three key elements—Prayer, Study and Work—allowing monks to develop key virtues in a simple pattern, practice, and regular routine in order to maintain a peaceful quality to their lives and calling. To quote Ruth Hayley Barton from her book *Sacred Rhythms*, "A rule of life seeks to respond to two questions: Who do I want to be? How do I want to live? Actually, it might be more accurate to say that a rule of life seeks to address the interplay between these two questions: How do I want to live so I can be who I want to be?"

As we dove into understanding the rule of life at the Transforming Center, first set forth by Saint Benedict, we were encouraged at the end of our two-year journey to begin creating our own rule of life for ourselves. And while I deeply appreciate the framework laid out by Saint Benedict, I realized that what I needed was something that stretched a bit further. A rule of life that would encompass not only my being but also my doing. As human beings, we all derive something important from the "doing" part of our lives. This book is not a call to throw away "doing." It is a call to align our "being" first and then through the lens of who we are created to be, we find our "doing." This is where we must decide what matters most and from that place internal place of rest form the new way of doing.

"How do I want to live so I can be who I want to be?"

—Ruth Haley Barton

That is when I began to explore what it would mean to create a more *Modern Day Rule of Life* for myself. A rule that would gather and honor the elements of the ancient rule but that would also add in the elements of the important forward movement of how we live and move in the world today.

As I was working to form and articulate my own rule of life, these two key life verses began to guide me.

In Romans 12:1–2 (MSG), the apostle Paul exhorts us in this way: "So here's what I want you to do, God helping you: Take your everyday, ordinary life—your sleeping, eating, going-to-work, and walking-around life—and place it before God as an offering. Embracing what God does for you is the best thing you can do for him. Don't become so well-adjusted to your culture that you fit into it without even thinking. Instead, fix your attention on God. You'll be changed from the inside out. Readily recognize what he wants from you, and quickly respond to it. Unlike the culture around you, always dragging you down to its level of immaturity, God brings the best out of you, develops well-formed maturity in you."

Do you see that? We are called to take our everyday, ordinary life and place it before God, to renew our minds daily by offering up to Him our doing based on who we are, who God has created us to be. That particular passage has become the "why" behind the reason to create *a Modern Day Rule of Life* for myself. We all need a guide, something that pertains to our life and that gives us a map or a guide so that we can live into our ordinary days and create the extraordinary life that God is calling each of us to create.

Then in 2 Corinthians 4:16-18 (The Message) we read, "So we're not giving up. How could we! Even though on the outside it often looks like things are falling apart on us, on the inside, where God is making new life, not a day goes by without his unfolding grace. These hard times are small potatoes compared to the coming good times, the lavish celebration prepared for us. There's far more here than meets the eye. The things we see now are here today, gone tomorrow. But the things we can't see now will last forever."

I remember when Rory shared this passage with me and how it challenged me to realize that God is calling us to the things that are unseen and to not become fixated on only the things we can see. He is calling us to make forward movement in who we are "being" and what we are "doing"—purposeful doing and being in the areas that matter to us and that Christ calls us to work in.

It was with this thought that I began to create a process for a *Modern Day Rule of Life* that would encompass my being, my doing and bring harmony and rest to the once chaotic mess of my inner life.

Creating a *Modern Day Rule of Life*

Most of us have a rule of life whether we realize it or not. We are living in certain patterns of behavior, rhythms, and routines every single day. That doesn't always mean it is a healthy or positive pattern or behavior, but each of us has our own way of living our life through our thoughts, feelings, actions, and reactions. Many popular authors have written books filled with examples of both corporate and personal rules of life such as Michael Hyatt and Daniel Harkavy and their work through their book *Living Forward.* This book suggests designing a life with the end in mind, determining in advance the outcomes we desire and the path we need to follow to get there. Or my friend Dan Miller, author of *48*

Days to the Work You Love, who challenges entrepreneurs from all walks of life to create a life plan and translate it into meaningful, satisfying daily work. Or Peter Scazzero, who defines it this way in his book *Emotionally Healthy Spirituality*: "A Rule of Life, very simply, is an intentional, conscious plan to keep God at the center of everything we do."

From our faith traditions, we find many people have had their own rule of life such as Thomas Merton, Dorothy Day, and Martin Luther King Jr., who himself had a rule of life that he crafted and which consisted of 10 different principles. These 10 different principles were Martin Luther King's guiding principles and principles that he asked any demonstrator who wanted to march with him to commit to as well. Dallas Willard, an American philosopher, put it this way in the foreword of Trevor Hudson's book, *The Serenity Prayer*: "We have to find a central focus that pulls together the scattered fragments and shredded fringes of a life as we must live it.... We skip from thing to thing and are drawn in many directions of pleasure and grief."

In other words, instead of skipping all over the place and being scattered from thing to thing, we have an opportunity to sit and discern and decide the way we want to order and align our days so we can bring life instead of chaos.

"In Christian tradition there is a name for a way of life that moves us beyond random and haphazard approaches to a more intentional approach that allows us to say yes to our heart's deepest spiritual longings day in and day out. It is called a 'rule of life,' and it is simply a way of ordering our lives around the values, practices, and relationships that keep us open and available for God's mysterious work of transformation in our lives. A rule of life provides structure and space for our growth."

—Ruth Haley Barton "Sacred Rhythms"

In my own journey, as I learned what it meant to craft a *Modern Day Rule of Life* for myself, what started coming together now make up the components and tools of the REALIFE Process. The process is made up of several signature tools and four distinct components that I, and my team, coach and now certify others in today. These signature tools and four components of the REALIFE Process are what we will deep dive into in the next several chapters.

Before we go any further though, I must ask you: Are you ready? Is it time to settle down the chaos of river water that is shaken up in your life? Are you ready to explore what it might feel like to think differently and act and react differently? To stop living from a place of external rush and begin to lean into the feeling of internal rest. No more hair on fire! I realize that the REALIFE Process is not for everyone, and that is ok. However, if like me, you are feeling like shaken river water and are ready to settle into new behaviors, rhythms, and routines, then I invite you to read on to the next chapters. Let's deep dive together!

Before you move on to the next chapter, I encourage you to download our FREE REALIFE Process Workbook to guide you through the four components of the REALIFE Process. You can find the free workbook at therealifeprocess.com/bookresources.

"A Modern Day Rule of Life gives you structure to grow around, similar to how a trellis holds the vine."

THE PROCESS

CHAPTER 4

REALIFE Being™ – Component One

"He didn't mind how he looked to other people, because the nursery magic had made him Real, and when you are Real shabbiness doesn't matter."

–Margery Williams Bianco, *The Velveteen Rabbit*

Hello. My name is Teresa and I am a workaholic …

In 2015, when I decided to resign from my ministry position at the church, it was so that I could come home to be more present for my family and available to help Dale on the farm. It had been a hard blow to know that Eric was not going to be the help his dad needed anytime soon. With Eric's stints in and out of jail because of his drug addiction and his time in and out of rehab, he just wasn't able to be as reliable and able-bodied as Dale needed.

And while farm work kept me busy, it was seasonal in nature, and there was this itch to continue challenging myself in new ways. With my training and background in computers, I began working for a company as a remote virtual assistant. It really was the best of both worlds because it allowed me to stay present for Dale on the farm, and yet I didn't have to travel off the farm every day to do my work. I was beginning to practice choosing differently in my life and moving toward rest, not rush.

Before long I was serving five clients, which along with helping Dale, kept my plate full. Some of the best things about working with these five clients were the relationships I was privileged to build as I served them. One client in particular impacted me greatly, and we connected deeply around his God story and the similarities of our paths. Matt and his wife are fellow believers, and they were also adopting a daughter internationally from Russia. However, the more I worked with him, the more I also began to notice that he was struggling with workaholism, just like I was. One particular day, as I was having a conversation with Matt, he paused and said, "Teresa, you know something? You're not just a virtual assistant. You're actually a coach."

It was in that moment that a seed was planted. During the last two years of my training at the Transforming Center, as I worked on mapping out my first rule of life, I kept feeling like I wanted to move into something different from ministry. I wanted to help people in a different way than I had before. I was the master of living with my hair on fire, and it was becoming easier and easier to see it in others, especially the clients I now worked with as a virtual assistant.

I knew that through my own struggles and those of my clients, it always seemed to be about productivity and how much we could produce. But that formula wasn't working for me, much less the clients, like Matt, that I was working for. I knew that somehow it was time to live from a different place, a place of rest and not rush. That conversation with Matt, and the subsequent seed that was planted, would launch me into discovering what it meant to coach others and help them craft a different way of living their real life. A life that wasn't about producing more stuff or checking off one more box, but a life where the things that mattered most to them could rise to the top, where their real selves could breathe and find life again at a manageable, life-giving pace.

REALIFE in Real Life

In the beginning of 2021, I found myself in a place of overwhelm. I felt like I had so many responsibilities. Because I had learned a lot about myself through the Enneagram, I recognized my mindset and feelings with how I approached my business. Specifically, I recognized that I had been performing all of the pieces in my business and needed to stop resisting getting help.

Working through the Enneagram and REALIFE Process, I realized that I could accomplish more for the client while saving significant time and increasing my joy by hiring someone to help me with the first draft of writing projects. I would put together an outline of what I needed and record a short video explaining the project. Then, the writer would send me back a well-done first draft that saved me hours and put me in a place of joy. I no longer had to perform the energy draining work of completing the first draft. I only had to write an outline, record a short explainer video, and tweak or shape the draft to finalize it.

I continue to benefit daily from having learned about myself and viewing my doing and being through lens of the REALIFE Process.

—Elizabeth Cook, Client

Exploring this idea of coaching, in 2016 I enrolled in the Professional Christian Coaching Institute (PCCI) in order to learn and become certified as a coach. It would take me three years to finish the certification course, but I learned so much in this coach training that would prepare me for what was to come next. During that time, I also listened to a podcast by Chris McCluskey (the founder and president of PCCI) and Kim Avery, a current instructor and cohost of the podcast *Professional Christian Coaching Today*, where they talked about the book *The 12 Week Year: Get More Done in 12 Weeks than Others Do in 12 Months.* The ideas and concept intrigued me, and I wondered if maybe this could be a tool for my clients. I had always been drawn to systems and processes, and this might be the tool I could use to build my coaching business. This might be the "something" I was looking for to help order my life. When I discovered that there was training for the 12 Week Year system, I jumped in with both feet. However, while it was a great program and I loved the overall concept, I just kept feeling like there was still a better process to capture my desire to live life differently. A process where the model was not just about productivity and getting things done from striving. A process that combined the idea that we can be successful and do the work God has for us today without being so driven by workaholism, the need for affirmations, and the empty success of checked-off to-do lists.

It was while I was wrestling with building out my own 12 Week Year Plan that I had set up a call with Natalie Eckdahl, the founder and president of BizChix, a successful coaching business geared toward women entrepreneurs. I had this particular call scheduled on my calendar for weeks, and yet, just prior to the actual call, our world was turned upside down with Eric's passing in August of 2017. In the weeks that followed Eric's funeral, there was so much we were processing and grieving. I debated canceling the call, but at the last minute, I decided to follow through with it, from my car no less. That day I was on my way to lead a women's spiritual retreat and pulled into a local McDonald's so I could have Wi-Fi for the call. I was so thankful for the privacy of my car as the tears flowed during that conversation. Today I can't express just how glad I was that I decided to stop and take that call.

That day as I shared with Natalie about the direction I felt drawn to, working hard to take these systems I had learned through the 12 week Year Coaching Certification course, striving to build it into something of substance, she said to me, "Teresa, you don't need to do someone else's program. You have one within you!" It was a God moment in my story and I realized that she was right. It was time to develop my own coaching process.

It was from that pivotal conversation that the REALIFE Process was born. Back then I didn't know what it might look like, but I was done trying to do everyone else's systems. It was time to start taking all I had learned from my time at the Transforming Center, the long conversations and lessons about crafting a rule of life for myself, and the spiritual disciplines and practices I had begun to embrace, and start crafting what today we call the REALIFE Process—the signature tools and the four components that make up the process. It was time to do what matters and live from rest, not rush, and truly pursue my life's work.

Beginning the Journey to REAL

In chapter 2, I talked about the moment when God used the story of *The Velveteen Rabbit* to start showing me ways to do the hard work to finally become real in my own life. Learning to be truly real was a journey that Eric had started prior to his passing and work that I am carrying on for myself and others in the years since his death. It is deep work, this becoming real. And that is the question I want to ask you: Are you ready to do the hard work of becoming real? Real to yourself and real to those who matter most to you? If so, I can tell you that it is a journey unlike any other. It takes great courage, and along the way some may question your motives, but the results will be life-changing.

Because of the journey I now show up differently, more authentic and present with Dale, my family, my friends, my clients, and with you, my reader. It took me a while to even realize that for myself, but after Eric passed and I began the coaching practice that I run today, I realized how true that had become of me.

I spent so many years running around with my hair on fire that any nod toward authenticity was lost in the whirl of doing and chasing success. Today though, this idea of being real, authentic, and present with people has become a part of my everyday language, and it is what I desire to invite people into. Inviting them to a deeper journey of being real—what that looks like for them individually because it's different for everyone—and how to embrace their authentic self.

Signature Tools for REAL Discovery

Earlier in the book, I had shared with you about crafting your own *Modern Day Rule of Life*. However, part of the process of crafting your own *Modern Day Rule of Life* is to begin to discover and uncover some of your current behaviors, rhythms, and routines so that you can start the process of developing new ones that align with your true self.

In developing the REALIFE Process, I have learned that when we do the work to discover what truly matters, we are leaning into who we are "being" not just what we are "doing," and that awareness allows us to work from a posture of rest.

Laying this important groundwork first allows you to truly become real, just like in the Velveteen Rabbit story I often refer to. I have found that using the signature tools that we have developed helps our coaching clients, and will help you as well, giving language and words to what we know deep in our being to be true. Having words to give to what we are thinking and feeling is so important and it's why we are drawn to processes and assessments that help us understand ourselves.

When I work with individuals and begin to address what it means to lean into Component One in the process, which we call REALIFE Being™, it is important that I start with coaching the whole person, not just one area or the other. There is something so powerful when you can really drill down and give language to something inside you and be truly authentic.

That is why, in the REALIFE Process, we start out by inviting you to discover three of our signature self-discovery tools before you ever begin to craft your *Modern Day Rule of Life*. To start, we always begin by talking about what needs and values are and what they are not.

The REALIFE Needs and Values Assessment™

The first of those tools is our signature REALIFE Needs and Values Assessment™. You can find an introduction to this tool on page 45 in the book and as a part of the downloadable resources at www.therealifeprocess.com/bookresources.

According to *Merriam-Webster*, *Need* is defined as "a situation in which someone or something must do or have something; something that is needed in order to live or succeed or be happy: a strong feeling that you must have or do something."

At the REALIFE Process, we believe that God is the supplier of all our needs. The Needs and Values tool is a way to gain perspective into what makes you unique. The purpose of this tool is to bring awareness to your predominant basic *Needs*. Knowing this, you can interact with God on a deeper level, expressing gratitude for met needs and asking Him to meet unmet needs. Identifying your *Needs* illuminates surrender and gratitude as you walk with God in your everyday, ordinary life.

Now, onto what needs are not. Needs are not wants; needs are what we must have to feel safe, grounded, and satisfied. Wants are different from needs; wants are the AND to needs. Needs are basic; wants are the icing on the cake! When your needs are met, you find that your wants list has less of a pull on you. Remember, wants are what you desire to have but could actually live without.

As you begin to work on your own REALIFE Needs and Values Assessment list, I encourage you to start paying attention to where those needs are showing up in your everyday, ordinary life: What needs are being met? What needs feel unmet and maybe need additional space in order to be met? When those needs and wants show up, I challenge you to capture them somewhere in writing so that you can come back and reference them.

I also encourage you to bring someone else into the process. Someone you trust but who can also give you feedback on what you are starting to identify. When I was first working through my REALIFE Needs and Values Assessment, I invited my husband, Dale, to join me in the process by filling out his own assessment. By working together and individually on the assessment, it became a great communication tool for both of us, causing us to learn so much more about one another along the way even after 40 years of marriage. You could use a coach or a mentor or a close friend as your sounding board. For those who have gone through the REALIFE Process with me or one of our coaches or facilitators, many have expressed how helpful it has been to say these things out loud.

Now that we have talked about needs, let's take a look at *Values*. *Values* are who you are. That is, once your basic needs are met, you tend to want to express your values.

"Once you have a clear picture of your priorities—that is your values, goals and high leverage activities—organize around them."

—Stephen Covey

Keep in mind that *Values* are not needs. If you need something, it is not a value, even though it may appear to be. Once you experience your needs being satisfied and met, you see this distinction more clearly between your needs and how those intersect with the unique values that God has given to you.

Remember, values are what you do or how you express yourself after your needs are met.

To illustrate this through a REALIFE example, I want to introduce you to Elizabeth Simmons, one of our *REALIFE Process Certified Facilitators*, who shared her experience and discoveries about herself as she went through this exercise early in the REALIFE Process:

> I need and value freedom. Yet, through the Process, I've uncovered the realization that I also need guardrails. If left to my own devices, I am scattered, disorganized, and, even, at times, shallow and not staying present because I'm looking ahead to the next fun thing or idea. The REALIFE Process has helped me slow down, pay attention to what I need and to leave margin for stillness and solitude: two things I've never desired, until now. Guardrails. Every 90 days, I revisit and reset: I look at my REALIFE Needs and Values

and determine if they are being reflected in my decisions; I choose new Projects to focus on; I also check to see if I'm being intentional with my time by including the people who are life-giving to me. Guardrails may sound confining for some, but for me, it gives me freedom to slow down, to listen to God, spend time with family and the people I love, run my business efficiently and to do the things that really matter, and to do them well.

As you work through the Intro to REALIFE Needs and Values Assessment™ and you identify your top five needs, you might do some writing around these three questions:

- What did you notice about your top needs?
- How are your needs met?
- What needs are a priority but are unmet?

In the same way, list out your top five values and reflect on the following questions through writing down these thoughts:

- What awareness did you gain from seeing your top values?
- How do you currently live out your values in your everyday life?
- What would shift if you were to honor those values?

Intro to REALIFE Needs & Values™

Read through the list of Needs & Values and list your top 5 of each below.

NEEDS

Acceptance
Accomplishment
Acknowledged
Be Loved
Be Right
Be Cared For
Certainty
Comfort
Communicate
Control
Be Needed
Duty
Freedom
Honesty
Order
Peace
Power
Recognition
Safety
Work

VALUES

Adventure
Beauty
Catalyst
Contribute
Creativity
Discovery
Feelings
Leadership
Mastery
Pleasure
Relatedness
Sensitivity
Spirituality
Teaching
Winning

My Top 5 Needs:

____

____

____

____

____

My Top 5 Values:

____

____

____

____

____

While you are writing, reflect on where you see God working, the things He is pointing out, and how it relates to your story, both past and present, because remember, your story matters. As you work through your needs and values, it will begin to help you see where you are or are not showing up in your life, what things are or are not important to you, how you are wired, and what might shift if you were to honor those values.**

This REALIFE Needs and Values Assessment is one of the ways you can start getting to the heart of who you are and who God has created you to be. This is a starting place for where you can begin to lean into your first component of the REALIFE Being™.

Erica Vinson, the director of the REALIFE Facilitator Network™ and a *REALIFE Process® Certified Coach*, shares just how the REALIFE Needs and Values Assessment helped her see her worth and start down the road to becoming real and authentic during one of the REALIFE Process team retreats. In her words:

> I discovered that my top need was for communication and specifically the need to be heard. Bringing light to that need created awareness of the magnitude of moments from my childhood and into my adult years when my voice had been silenced.
>
> If my number one need was not being met, then how was that affecting how I was showing up in my life? The realization helped me understand my "REALIFE VIEW"—how I was seeing the world, the moments I had pushed down my emotions and played small for the sake of peace.
>
> Beyond the discovery was also an invitation to reclaim my voice. I came to understand that communicating and being heard was and is a real need that I can lean in to in order to show up as my best authentic self. I need to be in rela-

> tionships that allow me to be free to speak, to be assertive in a gracious but frank way. I can be courageous and use my voice.

In the same way that Erica shared how working through the Needs and Values exercise helped her validate and rediscover the value of her own voice, Terri Johnson, our *REALIFE Process® Integrator* and one of our *REALIFE Process® Certified Coaches*, also shares how the assessment helped her truly honor her own needs and values.

> Working through the Needs and Values Assessment made me recognize that I have to honor those needs and values if I want to live wholeheartedly. I realized to best honor those needs and values, it was important to plan adventure and risk. In the past when I didn't honor those parts of myself, I would become impulsive and jump into adventure and take risks that were not necessarily healthy. Understanding my desire for communication, honesty, and integrity in my own life has continued to help me craft my life in ways that honor that. It also helps me in choosing who I surround myself with so my needs and values are met, in particular around my own ongoing recovery work as a recovering alcoholic and drug addict.

These are just two examples of ways others have leaned into becoming more authentic and real in their own lives and the impact it has on their life and work today. In the same way, as you work at identifying your own needs and values, you can expect it to have an ongoing impact on who you are being and what actions you are taking as you apply all the components of the process together.

Now that we have introduced you to the REALIFE Needs and Values Assessment , let's take a look at a second tool that will help you continue to dig deeper into your real self—the tool of the Enneagram.

The REALIFE ENNEAGRAM Personality Profile™

I was first introduced to the Enneagram during my involvement with the Transforming Center. The Enneagram wasn't something I had heard of before, but because of my then addiction to anything in the "self-help" category, I was immediately drawn to it.

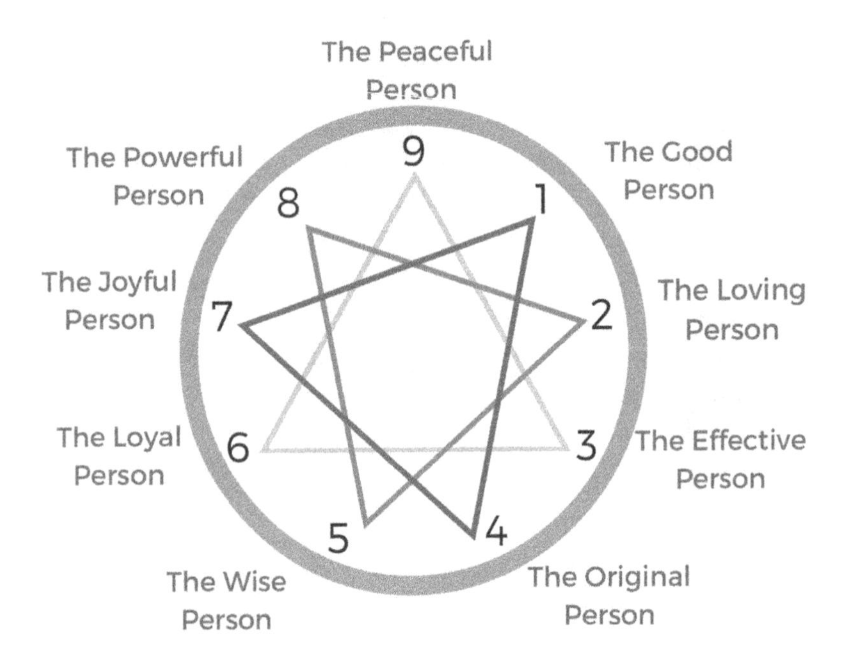

However, I quickly learned that the Enneagram was not a self-help tool at all but rather a tool for continued self-understanding. When I was introduced to the tool, it was actually through the spiritual practice of the Examen. To this day, the tool of the Enneagram has become one of the most helpful ways for me to see the deeper part of who I am. Not only has it been helpful in discovering my false self but more importantly it has helped me discover my true self. The real self that God intends for me to be.

As a musician, I relate well to one of my Enneagram mentors and certified Enneagram instructor Clare Loughrige. Here is an excerpt from an introduction to a book she coauthored with her husband, Scott, and certified Enneagram instructors Adele and Doug Calhoun.

> The Enneagram opens you to an extraordinary view to the truth about you. It can help you recognize your unique melody as well as where you are off-key internally and relationally. The Enneagram reveals your tempos, soloist agendas and dedication to your "playlist." Still discovering the truth of your number can never encompass who you are. Nor does it automatically change you or your relationships. Relational repairs and healthy interactions take intention and attention. Enneagram insights have to be applied to the rhythms and grooves of ordinary daily lives to bring transformation and harmony. —*Spiritual Rhythms for the Enneagram*

Through the use of the Enneagram, I have been able to discover patterns of behaviors, healthy and unhealthy, that have formed in my life. In turn, it has helped me to understand how God sees me uniquely from how I used to view myself.

Clare was instrumental in helping me to see that the Enneagram comes full circle when we view it through the use of the Enneagram Harmony Model. This model opened my eyes to the idea of the three centers of intelligence that reside in all of us.

The three centers of intelligence revolve around the following:

- The Heart Center or EQ Center

- The Head Center or IQ Center
- The Gut Intelligence or GQ Center

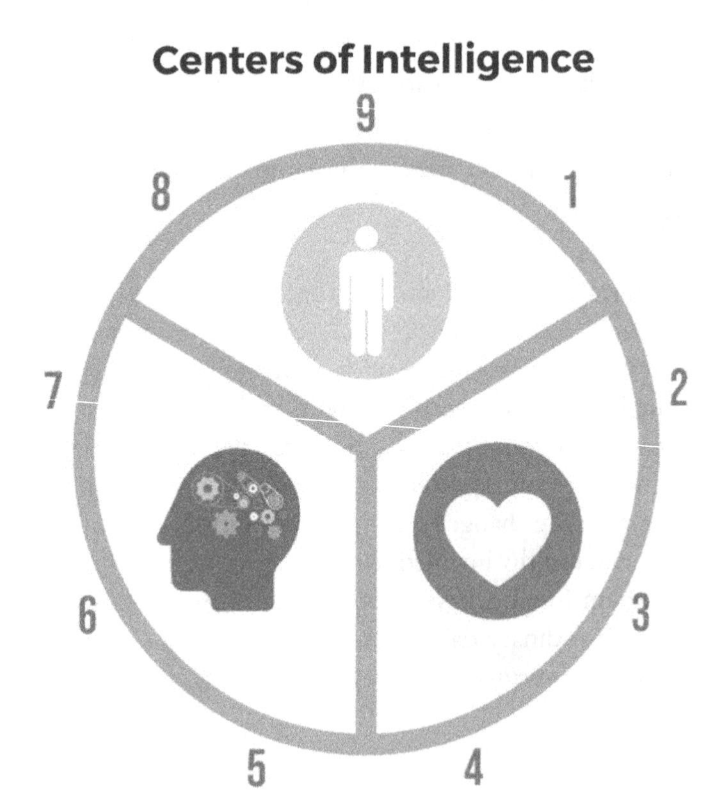

When I first saw this Harmony Model diagram of the Enneagram, I immediately was drawn to the simplicity. I was also drawn to the depth of wisdom that was within this particular Enneagram model. It felt so true and authentic and resonated deeply with me.

While the tool of the Enneagram is not scriptural, I do believe there are references to these three centers of intelligence in passages such as that found in Matthew 22:37 NIV, which says "Love the Lord your God with all your heart and with all your soul and with all your mind."

For my clients, learning the tool of the Enneagram and their connection to one of the nine Enneagram personality types, and how it ties to their own complete Harmony Triad, has been transformational.

Often my clients will discover places in these three centers that have been shut down similar to a water faucet that has been shut off for a long time. It could be that their emotional center has been shut off and they don't know how to process shame or sorrow in a healthy way. Or their Head Center has been shut off and everything is processed through fear, so they tend to overthink everything, like a hamster on the wheel. Or maybe they are very disconnected from their body or gut instinct, and in return, they either over process anger very outwardly or don't process it at all in order to keep the peace and avoid conflict.

So much of who we are in our ego structure is formed in us in the early and young adult years. This formation happens through nature—the gene pool we were given. Nurture—those who had influence in our formative years such as parents, family members, siblings, and teachers. And our own freewill choices. As children and young adults, this can be too much to process, so we do the best we can with what we know at the time. However, many times we turn things off or shut them down, leading to an unhealthy self. Turning back on all the faucets and working on the repairs allows thoughts, feelings, actions, or reactions to flow from these centers once again.

Waking up to all this awareness can bring such freedom and full-circle harmony movement for people into their true self and all that God created them to be. It is often the very beginning of living into their best REALIFE.

The Enneagram helps us to put language to the things that are deep within our soul. For example, as an Enneagram Type 3, I can be driven by a desire for success and performance. Notably these things have been a part of my story for as long as I can remember. From the early years and well into adulthood, there was always this crazy tape in my head that played over and over again, reinforcing the message that I was not enough.

The Harmony Enneagram helped me to see that God sees me as effective and efficient, and that is one of the gifts I bring to the world around me. However, if I overdo it in this area, it can lead to a performance-driven state of being.

When I put these gifts together with my Harmony connection to the Type 6—my Head Center—it brings faithfulness, while my Type 9 space brings peace. Leaning into all three centers allows me to move full circle, thus being fully present to my everyday, ordinary life and helping me to create a mantra or breath prayer that goes like this—I am a calm, loyal and effective daughter of God. Wow, what a wonderful place I can lean into every day.

Unfortunately, we don't have enough space in this book to really dive deep into the Enneagram. However, I would like to invite you to discover more by downloading the free REALIFE Process® Enneagram Typing Guide. This guide is an introduction to the full REALIFE ENNEAGRAM Personality Profile that is available as a resource on our website at therealifeprocess.com.

We also have references to some great resources at realifeprocess.com/bookresources. Many of our coaches and certified facilitators are also trained to work with the tool of the Enneagram, and you can find them on our website as well.

REALIFE in Real Life

My husband recently got a job offer that would have required us to move our family to Arizona. It was a really good offer, but there was some risk involved. We weren't really sure what to do, so we pulled out our Needs and Values materials, reviewed together and then pulled out our Enneagram resources and explored how we were evaluating the offer.

By doing so, we were able to check in with our heart and our gut, not just our head, to determine what the best decision would be and whether we were approaching the decision from the right place.

I could tell that my gut was telling me to do something, but my heart and my head were telling me something different. In the end, we decided not to take the job because we realized that the job, even though it would have been great financially, wouldn't meet our values or give us the direction that we want in life.

It was really helpful to know that our decision came from a whole-body, whole-self response. In the end, we felt complete peace and contentment with our decision. Even though we passed up what appeared to be an amazing offer, we know the decision came from the right place, from a whole-self place.

—Rebecca Cook, *REALIFE Process Certified Facilitator*

No Ordinary Pickles

Along with the mason jar of creek water I have sitting on my desk that I mentioned earlier in the book, I also have a jar of pickles. However, these are no ordinary pickles that you find at the store. In fact, these are pickles that I personally canned myself. One of the things you'll learn about me is that I love to garden, and putting up the produce from my yearly summertime labor brings me wonderful delight.

So why the jar of pickles on my desk? Well, have you ever heard of the rocks in the jar illustration? The illustration where you have a jar, some large rocks, some small pebbles, sand and then water? If so, then the concept is very much the same.

Our life is like a jar, and we all have an opportunity to fill it with a lot of things. However, it matters what order you put things into your jar. If you try to put in the water and sand first, adding the pebbles and then the large stones last, there's no way to fit it all. In fact, placed in the wrong order, you just end up spilling water everywhere and becoming frustrated at the lack of space in the jar.

It's the same with canning pickles. When I fill the mason jar with the hot sweet juice, from my mother-in-law's sweet pickle recipe, and then try to put the pickle slices, I can easily end up with a sticky mess all over my kitchen counter. However, if I add in the cucumber first and then pour in sweet juice, the juice flows around the pickles and it all belongs in the jar. Even leaving room in the jar for headspace! Without the one inch of headspace in a canning jar, you risk blowing the lid off the jar under pressure.

Just like the jar of creek water, my jar of pickles reminds me that I must start with the big pieces of my life that matter to me and then allow the other things flow around the most important aspects of my life. The headspace in the jar also reminds me that I need to allow for margin in my life. In fact, margin is the thing that most of us are not allowing enough of. We pack our lives fuller and fuller until we are living at a pace that is full-on rush!

Using what we have already discovered through the first two signature tools of the REALIFE Needs and Values Assessment and the REALIFE ENNEAGRAM Personality Profile, I'd like to introduce you to one more exercise and foundational tool we use at the REALIFE Process.

The REALIFE Process Mindmap™

This exercise and foundational tool helps our clients think outside the box and creatively brainstorm possibilities. We call it the REALIFE Process Mindmap™. Keep in mind that a mindmap is not linear; it allows your brain to engage in different ways by creating a way for ideas to flow more freely without the restriction of putting things in a sequential order.

When you look at this illustration, all you see are circles, but these circles are so helpful in allowing us to get our ideas chaptered into a visual place where we can process them differently in our brain. Many of us are highly visual learners, and the simple process of filling in the circles with words or thoughts allows us to gather them in a different order and see them through a new lens as I like to say.

the REALIFE Mindmap™

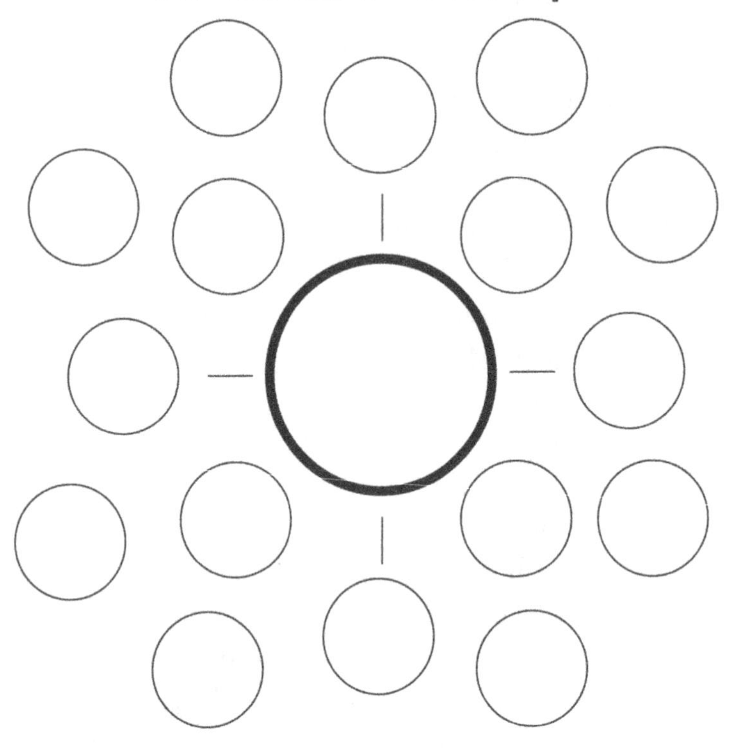

Mindmaps are often created around a single concept, drawn as an image in the center of a blank page. Associated representations of ideas are added, such as images, words, and parts of words. Major ideas are connected directly to the central concept, and other ideas branch out from those.

When I was first introduced to using a mindmap, it was so freeing. Mind mapping allowed me to stop thinking about what I needed to do first to be effective and instead allowed me to think creatively and just brain dump my ideas on paper.

My clients find such value in using a REALIFE Process Mindmap to begin thinking outside the box before gathering those thoughts into lists, projects, or action steps. Who knew that drawing circles on a piece of paper or a napkin could be so freeing? I've included an example of a REALIFE Process Mindmap here, and these worksheets are also available as part of the free resources you can download.

These three signature tools are so helpful as you begin to really dive into this first component of REALIFE Being™, capturing your real self and who you want to be BEFORE you move on to what you want to do. By considering your unique enneagram personality and your own personal Needs and Values, you can then begin to use the Mindmap tool to discover the key *Areas of Focus* for your life.

The REALIFE Process AREAS OF FOCUS™

In order to discover your own key *Areas of Focus*, let's begin by completing the following REALIFE Process Mindmap exercise: Using a piece of paper, draw a circle in the center and write "my life" in the center of the circle. Then consider the four to five key areas in your life that you would like to focus on and give priority to.

Some possible Areas of Focus could include the following: Spiritual, friendships, spouse, recreation, environment, financial, children, extended family, hobbies, education, health, professional, travel, self-care, or experiences.

The great part is that you get to choose and you get to give them a name. This is your REALIFE that you are defining. This is a part of crafting your *Modern Day Rule of Life*. By identifying these areas, it allows you to clear the clutter and stop chasing all the things. Naming what areas of your life really matter lets you take a big breath and say yes, and that big breath allows you the space to begin to slowly rest. Through the use of the tool of the Enneagram, the Needs and Values Assessment, and the REALIFE Process Mindmap around key Areas of Focus, what starts to come together is what I identify as your written compass, your very own REALIFE VIEW Document™.

The REALIFE VIEW Document™

Through each tool and exercise you do, you are beginning to walk through this first component in the process, your REALIFE Being; it is a process to discover who we truly are and what we truly want to pursue, and for that reason, we want to make sure we capture all that we are discovering in written form. You are now beginning to craft the "being" part of your *Modern Day Rule of Life*.

To begin to fill in your own personal REALIFE VIEW Document™, you can go to www.therealifeprocess.com/bookresources and download all the FREE resources and signature tools we have mentioned so far in the book as well as other helpful tools.

You will use the REALIFE VIEW Document to continue to craft out your *Modern Day Rule of Life* as we walk through the other three components of the REALIFE Process. This document will become the framework and map to guide you in your new way of being so you can live out your REALWORK in the world.

I encourage you to capture what you have discovered so far either on our REALIFE VIEW Document worksheet or in your own digital or written form. We capture these in sections on our downloadable form.

Section 1: Your REALIFE Needs and Values results from your assessment.

Section 2: Your Talents, Gifts, and Abilities—things you already know about yourself from other assessments, or things that you know to be true in your behavior, rhythms, and routines.

Section 3: Your REALIFE Statement—a personal mission statement for your life. Complete the following statement "I want my life to be about (fill in the blank with characteristics, talents, and abilities) by doing (fill in the blank with actionable items)" then combine the two statements to form your REALIFE Statement.

Here is my own personal REALIFE Statement:

Embracing each extraordinary day as an offering to God by being a bold, generous leader and creator. Encouraging and equipping others to discover their true REALSELF, manage their everyday REALIFE, and live out their calling to their REALWORK.

Section 4: Your Personal 5–7 Areas of Focus including your written I Am statement for each area of your life.

These are the four sections of the "Being" side of your REALIFE VIEW Document. I see such great power and ownership take place when this document is created and written down. It's not the structure of the document that's magic but the process of working through each section and pre-deciding what matters for your life. You will revisit this document often as you live out your new *Modern Day Rule of Life* and your REALIFE Process.

When you first get started with this process, you might realize that you are still trying to put too much into your pickle jar. It's at this point that you have to decide what is most important to focus on first. Realize that in order to remain healthy you can only focus well on a handful of areas at one time.

Once you identify your five to seven Areas of Focus and have written them down in your REALIFE VIEW Document, I encourage you to write an Area of Focus Statement for each one. Keep in mind that you want to write it as an I Am Statement. By writing it as an I Am Statement, you are focusing on how you will ideally be living out that value in the future.

For example, here is one of my personal "I am" focused statements: "I am prioritizing my health and exercising four to five days a week." Even though I am not living that reality currently, this is my desire in the next one to two years. By writing this as an I Am Statement, it helps me to identify where I want to go.

The true value of the statement is writing it based on where you want to be in that area of your life in the next year or two at the most. For most of my clients, I find that about a year is a good time frame to look toward in the future. Why? Because most people are leaning into a new routine and rewriting those statements to fit their current growth regularly through discernment. It's not that the Area of Focus has changed, but through continued self-discovery and growth and living more authentically, they are coming back and revisiting their *Modern Day Rule of Life*. However, remember, you get to decide how often you update these statements because this is your REALIFE and your own personal I Am Statements, not anyone else's.

Here are a few other I Am Statements written by past clients or *REALIFE Process Certified Facilitators*:

Area of Focus – Family & Friends: "I sow into building deeper relationships and connections by being a vulnerable and available friend."

Area of Focus – Self-Care: "I regularly journal, walk, and engage in meaningful conversation with my closest friends. This is energizing and grounding for me."

Area of Focus – Trusting Faith: "I am intimately connected to the heart of God and deeply loved by Him. We do life together and share His love everywhere we go."

Area of Focus – Professional: "I am an influencer and entrepreneur growing a multiple six-figure business as a coach, podcaster, speaker and author. I am influencing, serving, and equipping people through my company to live a sustainable *Modern Day Rule of Life*. I inspire them to live extraordinary lives through the coaching and training I provide, the content I create, retreats I host, and speaking I do."

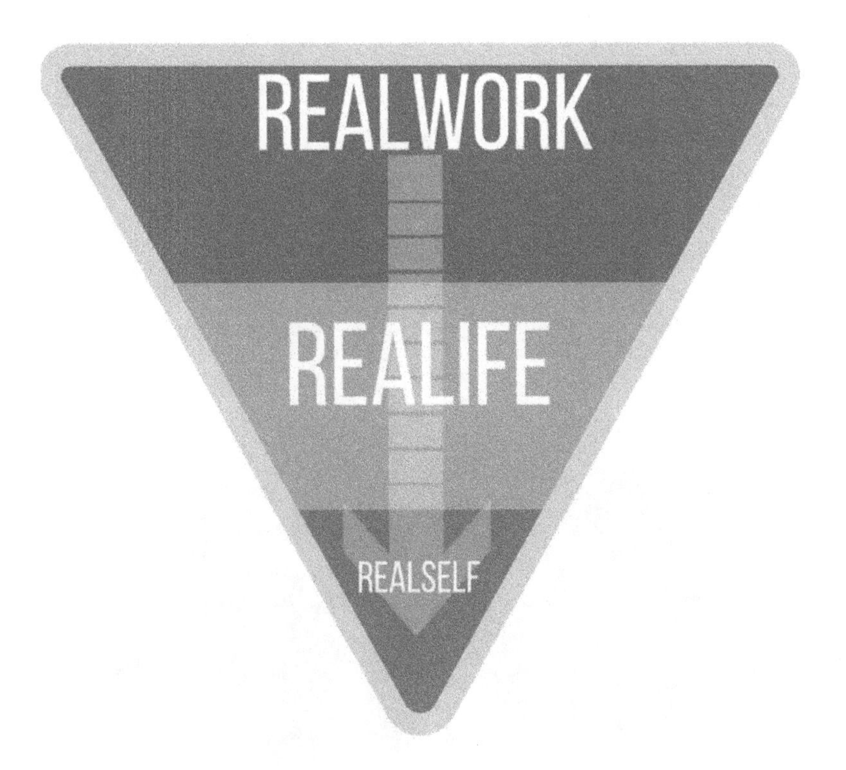

This upside-down triangle represented my life several years ago when I was living from a state of rush with my hair on fire. It was me before I really started doing the hard work of becoming real in my own life. The way I was living my life was all about my work, my success, my titles, and my achievements. With work being my central focus, it was what in turn flowed down into my REALIFE with my relationships, my family, my children, my husband, and my own inner person, and it didn't flow well.

This work focus took over who I was; it became my identity, taking over my time, my choices, and my calendar. It dictated how

I showed up in my life. At the end of the day, I had forgotten who I was and whose I was. I forgot that God had uniquely created me for the work He had for me to do.

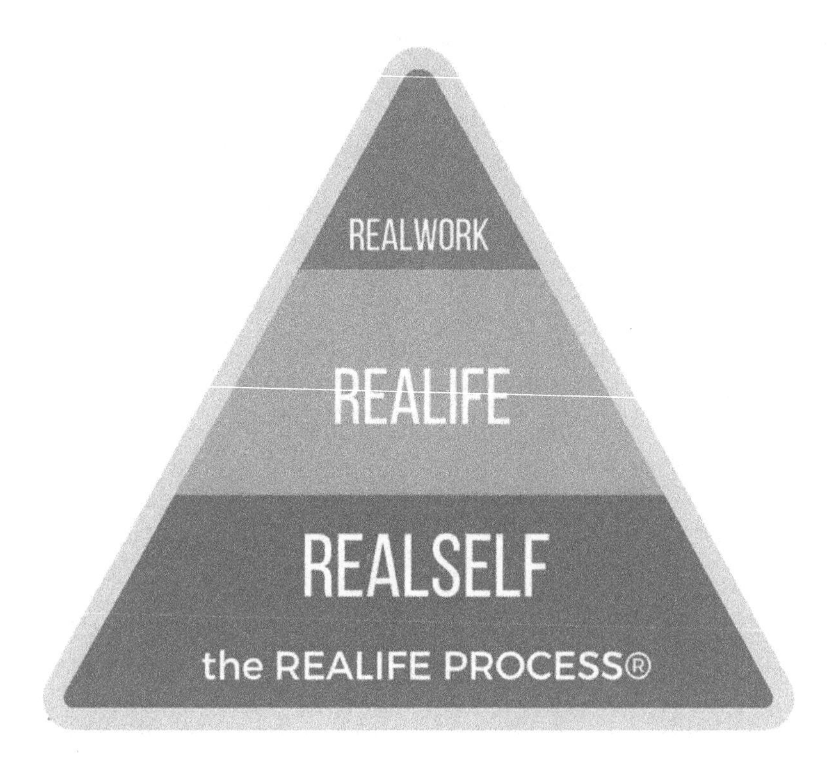

It was time to flip the triangle. I had to work on who I was being before I thought about what I was doing. So many of us have been there and live that way, and it's slowly killing us, threatening our relationships and our work, and stealing our joy and contentment.

However, when we bathe our life in our being, who we are through all three centers of intelligence God has given us, what our needs and values are, and what we want our lives to focus on, then we are able to live more authentically to who we are.

It is important to remember though, that it is a journey of discovery that is made up of very slow and steady process. A process and path that needs a compass and a map to follow—a map we call the REALIFE VIEW Document.

This journey to our real and authentic self is about the long game. It is about creating our new *Modern Day Rule of Life.* In other words, this is a marathon and not a sprint. And yet it is a journey that along the way will allow you to ask questions that challenge you to look at how you manage your time and your commitments on your calendar, how you are showing up to relationships in your life, and so much more.

Doing this kind of process allows you to then manage your life in a more realistic way. Then you can truly move into the work that you are called to pursue—the work God has created and designed you to do.

Here's a fun tidbit. During my time at the Transforming Center, we were not allowed to introduce ourselves to others by what job or career we held. You know how hard it is to carry on a conversation with someone and not ask what they do for a career? And yet, it really made me slow down and think—to really tap into my own being and not my career title.

As you begin to shape and form your *Modern Day Rule of Life* around your behaviors, rhythms, and routines that you have discerned with God, you will begin to capture that in your own REALIFE VIEW Document.

In doing so you will begin to see how you can bring your being into your everyday, ordinary life, and I can't wait to help you bring that full circle in our next steps! Let's keep going!

BRING JOY

CHAPTER 5:

REALIFE Action™ – Component Two

> "'Does it hurt?' asked the Rabbit. 'Sometimes,' said the Skin Horse, for he was always truthful. 'When you are Real you don't mind being hurt.'"
>
> **—Margery Williams, *The Velveteen Rabbit***

After working in the coaching business from March of 2017 until April 2020, I had finally developed the four key components of the REALIFE Process, and it was going really well. I was coaching with individuals, holding workshops, presenting trainings, and working on developing my own keynotes for upcoming speaking engagements. It felt good and was proving to be a solid direction for my business. I had even added two team members to support the business.

In 2019 I had spoken at some fairly large events and was scheduled to speak at an even bigger event in April of 2020. Then in March of 2020, COVID-19 shut down everything. The entire world stopped for a bit and just took a breath. The shutdown meant no more in-person speaking engagements or other in-person events, and I had no idea when it would begin again.

It really felt like 2020 was going to be a breakout year for our business, but then COVID-19 hit, and with it, the uncertainty of the days ahead. It was discouraging because I felt I was just finding momentum with my business and my message. What now? I had to decide how to pivot. In deciding to pivot, I knew I had to really lean into my own process, relook at my Areas of Focus, in particular around my professional area. It meant revisiting the I Am Statement that I had written around my business and considering if it still held true or if I was going to need to rewrite a whole new statement in this Area of Focus in the current COVID-19 atmosphere.

Prior to COVID-19 shutting down the world, coaches and entrepreneurs that I worked with had begun to say, "I really like how you have your process laid out, with the content, signature tools, and done-for-you worksheets and the ways it helps people address first the 'being' of their lives and then the 'doing.'"

This statement was then often followed by the question: "Could I possibly use parts of your content for the work I am doing with my clients?"

Honestly, creating a program that would benefit other faith-focused entrepreneurs, coaches, and consultants had been in the back of my head for a while. However, I figured I wouldn't tackle that for the next few years at least. But when the shutdown came in March of 2020, I decided that my *Project* for Q2 would be to develop a beta test of our first version of the REALIFE Process Certification Program. (At that time, that is what we were calling it, a certification program. Today it is known as the REALIFE Facilitator Network with the first year being the certification process.)

I started by using a REALIFE Process Mindmap to lay out the Project and started talking to others and those I was working with about this new beta program. I also talked with those in my group coaching program and began to invite people to give the beta course a try. Along with talking and reaching out to my clients and network, I began to write out my *Action Steps*, those things I needed to do in order to pivot well and move forward in this new direction.

During this process, I remember a very specific conversation with one of my REALIFE Process team members and one of my best friends. I was sitting with them during a team meeting and presenting this new direction and beta test idea, and I remember asking, "What do you think? Can we do this?"

As I spoke about my new idea, they became as excited as I had become about the doors and possibilities this new direction might open for the REALIFE Process and those we were serving. So, as a team, we mind mapped around it, wrote out our *Action Steps*, and in the last weekend of May 2020, launched our beta test orientation group of what we now currently call the REALIFE Facilitator Network.

As of the writing of this book, we are now 20 months into that program, have over 32 *REALIFE Process Certified Facilitators*, 2 *REALIFE Process Certified Coaches*, and have successfully moved from the beta test of the program to a now fully launched REALIFE Facilitator Network, which is an ongoing network of certified facilitators who walk in life together both personally and professionally using the REALIFE Process as our foundational tool. So how was I able to make a successful pivot during a very uncertain and difficult time and take clear action? It honestly comes back to the things we just talked about in the previous chapter. I took the discovery of this new idea, brought it down into a REALIFE Process Mindmap, and started mapping out all the things

I thought were possible or the things I would need to do—the action I would need to take.

By mapping out the idea into clear and *Actionable Steps*, it allowed me to see the possibilities and the roadblocks and make steady progress forward. As I worked through my Action Steps, it was as simple as taking the right next step in my Project. Once I finished that step, I moved on to the next one and then the next one. Sometimes the steps are small, such as making a phone call or sending an email. That is how I, and you, can take your Areas of Focus and the things that matter to you and move them forward one small step at a time.

Often I am asked, "How do you get so much done?" And I do get a lot accomplished. As a Type 3 on the Enneagram, I can be very forward moving. However, it has less to do with my personality type and more to do with focusing on the very next best Action Steps in the Project I have chosen to work on in the next 90 days. While it may seem simple, I have learned to trust the process, and you can too! Let's take the next step together!

The Next Best Step

In chapter 4, we left off having worked through our REALIFE Needs and Values Assessment, discovering exactly what our needs and wants truly are. We also explored where our personalities fit in and line up through the use of the REALIFE ENNEAGRAM Personality Profile signature tool, hopefully leading to a greater understanding of who God has uniquely created us to be. Lastly, we worked through identifying our Areas of Focus by using the REALIFE Process Mindmap, identifying those areas of our life that are most important to us, both personally and professionally.

Using these signature tools is what then helps you begin to build out your REALIFE VIEW Document and ultimately your own everyday *Modern Day Rule of Life*.

So what's next?

Action! It's time to take all of those discoveries and start making forward progress and taking action in your own life.

Taking the *Areas of Focus,* the big rocks (or pickles) of your life, that you identified earlier, begin to place them into buckets or jars. For example, some of my buckets might be health, spiritual life, family, or work. Everybody's buckets are going to look different because they are based on YOUR Area of Focus in your life right now.

You will also want to be looking at your *Area of Focus Statements*—those I Am Statements that you wrote down for each of these Areas of Focus. From those Areas of Focus, you will begin to craft your specific Action Steps for each focus area.

Keep in mind though, that if you identified seven to eight Areas of Focus, the reality is that you should only focus on two to three of those areas over the next 90 days. Trying to focus on more than that will be overwhelming and lead to discouragement, lack of change, and little to no forward progress.

I often hear clients say they are overwhelmed. Usually the reason they feel so overwhelmed is that they believe they should be able to do it all at the same time. A better idea to live in harmony is to know that focusing on two to three Areas of Focus for 90 days is the best way to not feel overwhelmed. Work smarter not harder as they say. Forward energy creates momentum.

From my experience and that of others, focusing on only two to three areas at one time can truly help facilitate significant change and valuable progress in areas that really matter to you.

As an example of why focused attention on the right things matters, let me introduce you to my friend Mark Ross. Mark is a *REALIFE Process Certified Facilitator*, and several years ago he found himself in a bit of a quandary. Mark, at the time, was just a few years into starting, what he calls, his encore career in business coaching and in art. Both endeavors took up a fair amount of time, as any new adventure does.

Focusing on two to three **Areas of Focus** for 90 days is the best way to not feel overwhelmed.

However, about the same time that Mark was investing in his new business, he was also becoming more and more responsible for his aging parents. Both areas needed his attention and help, but the frustration came in not knowing how to juggle all the pieces of his business, life, and elder care at the same time.

For years, prior to his retirement, Mark had worked in an environment where he had other people to help shoulder the workload and day-to-day responsibilities, freeing him to juggle various things at once with no trouble. Fast forward to the present and the now solo effort of running his own business and shouldering all the responsibility. Mark realized that he needed a new skill set in this season of life.

> I realized that I needed some help and a way to identify what was important, what mattered the most, and how to actually get things done. Around that time, Teresa was offering a beta testing opportunity to the REALIFE Process and what she was developing there for others. I initially wondered how this could help me, but quickly I realized

> it offered a framework that resonated with me. I needed help to organize my calendar, build out my ideal week, and focus on what was important to me in the next 60–90 days. It also gave me the permission to let go of some things and really just focus on two to three things that were really important to me. It was a holistic approach to life and work that I really appreciated. By approaching my personal and professional life this way, it helped me find time to care for our parents, which I fondly came to call "the parent project." Identifying it this way helped me look at it objectively, and along with my work, I was able to do both by having a process that worked.

Mark, through identifying two to three *Areas of Focus*, which included care of his parents, was able to not only focus on these important Projects but also make significant progress forward to care for his parents well. Not only that, but he has continued to successfully build out his coaching practice and produce ongoing works of art.

That is the power of focusing on small Projects over time. So let's look at how you can begin to gain the same focus and forward momentum in what matters to you.

The Next 90 Days

As we dive deeper into this second component of the REALIFE Process—REALIFE Action™—we're going to start by creating 90-day actionable Projects to move forward in a few of these Areas of Focus. Ninety days is roughly three months of focused attention in these two to three key areas, making the Action Steps you put in place for these areas manageable and doable.

Sometimes those key areas are really obvious. For example, right now we are busy planning our daughter's wedding, which is coming up in the next few weeks. This is a big life event for us, and so I have made my daughter's wedding a Project in this particular 90 days.

In the same way, be sure to lean in and discern those big areas of your life that need attention in this season. Maybe, like me, you have a big life or family event you want to give attention to. Maybe there is a big shift you are making in your business that needs some direct attention, or you want to focus on key areas of your health in these 90 days. Whatever it is, remember that in 90 days you will be reevaluating the key areas of your life through a 90 DAY Reset™ that we will walk you through to see if there is a needed adjustment, addition, or possibly a continuation in that area.

By revisiting these areas every 90 days, it keeps us from getting out of harmony in our lives and making sure we are continually addressing all the key areas of our life and not avoiding other areas that need attention along the way.

In chapter 7, we will talk more about the 90 DAY Reset, but for now, just know we have a plan built into the process for these reviews. The REALIFE Process is a complete process and has resetting and reviewing these important pieces of our lives built in.

So how do you practically map out your Projects and the corresponding Action Steps for the first time?

First, you will want to pull out a piece of paper to start visually using the REALIFE Process Mindmap for the Area of Focus you have chosen to give attention to in the next 90 days. For example, say I want to focus on my health in the next 90 days; I would then draw one big circle in the middle of my paper and write the word "Health" in the center.

Next, take some time to brain dump on your Mindmap all the things about your health that you might want to address such as a visit to the dentist, yearly blood work, a massage, a visit to the chiropractor, or weekly trips to the gym. Anything that you think you want to focus on in regard to your health should be dumped out on the page.

Next, take a step back and look at everything you just dumped on the page that pertains to this important Area of Focus around your health. These may all be worthwhile things, but the reality is you can't necessarily address all of these areas around your health at once.

Bearing that in mind, narrow down a couple of key things around your health that you want to address in the next 90 days. For instance, maybe it is getting to the dentist and also seeing your chiropractor for a checkup.

Once you have made your Project choice, write down the key *Action Steps* that are needed to move forward. In this example, the key Actions would be to make the phone calls to schedule the needed appointments at the dentist and chiropractor and then follow up as needed. This is an example of a very simple Project, but it gives forward motion in the next 90 days toward the overall Area of Focus of your health.

That is why we call this second component of the process, REALIFE Action. It's vital that once you identify and discern Areas of Focus that you now take action to see those areas move forward in a healthy and holistic way. It's a simple but effective and repeatable process that will cause you to make great strides forward in your life while living a more harmonious process.

Now, repeat this second component with one to two more Areas of Focus and you are almost ready to move on to the next component. Remember, you're doing real life here. You're going to work, you're being with your spouse and your kids, and you're doing all the things while you're moving these small, actionable Projects forward with these Action Steps. In the next chapter, we are going to flesh out the third component of the process: how to find time to put these Projects in your everyday, ordinary life that is already very full.

Remember to also write out your Projects and Action Steps on the second page of your REALIFE VIEW Document that you can find in the downloadable resources.

Section 5: These Are My Projects and Action Steps for the Next 90 Days.

This is another important part of the map you are creating. You are now shifting to the doing and pursuing side of your new *Modern Day Rule of Life.* You are gaining momentum, and you want to capture what you are pre-deciding in your REALIFE VIEW Document. It's all starting to come together.

Projects versus Goals

I want to take a moment to talk about the word "Projects." As you might have noticed, I have been referring to the Actionable Steps around the key Areas of Focus as Projects and not as goals. While there is nothing inherently wrong with the word "goals," I personally prefer the term Projects when it comes to what I am focusing on in the next 90 days.

Why? Because to me shooting for a "goal" is something that we can easily fail at and then get discouraged. However, a "Project" is something it feels like we can work with and work within as we make forward progress. A Project allows us to adjust or add in an additional Action Step if needed. A "goal," especially a big, hairy audacious goal, is just out there and can hover over us.

Many times my clients feel huge relief when we change the language from goals to Projects. Words matter and can become a mental block or a catalyst for us. Within my REALIFE Process, the word goal would be more fitting with the I Am Statements that are written for each Area of Focus, and the word Project is breaking that goal statement into bite-size doing pieces.

So I love the word Projects. It just feels much more doable, and I find that that language resonates well for most people. However, whatever you call it—either goals or Projects—make sure you are being purposeful about writing down each individual Action Step and keep moving yourself forward.

"A vision without a plan is a pipe dream."

—Brian Moran, *The 12 Week Year*

Taking Action

When I first started working, back in 2015 and 2016, to create my own REALIFE VIEW Document and discover my own Areas of Focus, one of those key areas that kept coming up for me was how much I enjoyed and wanted to travel. Up until that point, even though I desired to travel, I had not made it a priority. So much had shifted and changed since Eric passed away and yet that longing to travel was still deep within me.

Yes, Dale and I had done some traveling earlier in our marriage to places like the Caribbean, our trip to pick up our daughter in Romania, and other places along the way. However, as Dale and I moved into our mid-fifties, I realized that I still desired to see so much more of the world than what we had done up until that point.

So one of my Areas of Focus is Travel & Recreation. Over time I have rewritten the I Am Statement for this area to what it currently is, and I have done many Projects around this particular area. During one of my early days with the process, I decided to make travel and recreation one of my Projects for 90 days. I spent time mind mapping around it and deciding on the Action Steps to see travel become a bigger part of our life. This kind of focus allows me to decide where we want to go, where we might want to stay, decide on our travel budget, and key in on specific trips we want to take. Along with travel, we also desired to do some type of hobby together. My I Am Statement then looked like this: "We are vacationing two to three weeks out of the year and participating in hobbies and recreation together."

I then broke that I Am Statement down into Projects with Actionable Steps so that over the past few years of us focusing on this area of our lives Dale and I have begun to live this reality of having travel be a big part of our lives.

It also helped to ask the following questions: Where do we want to go? What is on our bucket list? Do we want to rent condos? Do we want to fly to places and just stay in a hotel? By asking these kinds of questions, we were able to start identifying what kind of vacations we wanted to take and what the travel looked like for us. Sometimes we flew to destinations while other times we decided to drive.

Each one gave us a different experience but helped us to start identifying the way we like to take vacations and do recreation and relax together. We also identified times of the year that were better for us to travel versus other times. Because Dale farms, we know that during certain times of the year, we really need to be on the farm for planting and harvest. Bearing that in mind we don't schedule trips during key growing seasons but rather wait until the season is over and then take the often needed break together. This is part of learning and discerning how to live from rest, not rush.

We also identified a key hobby that we enjoy together, which is golfing. So guess what? Last year, for Christmas, we bought golf clubs for each other so that we could enjoy this hobby together when we vacation. By setting out that vision of what we wanted that key area of our lives to look like, we were able to break it down into Projects over time with Actionable Steps and really see that I Am Statement come to life.

You can see that this is a process that happens over time, and it is so much more than just Projects you are doing to check a box on your list. These Projects are helping to form new behaviors, rhythms, and routines that shape your life into a new *Modern Day Rule of Life* with a stronger and stronger trellis and beautiful growing vines that you plant, prune, and tend so that they flourish over time. I'll have more to say about that in chapter 9.

REALIFE in Real Life

In the past, I have struggled to set and keep goals. I would generally set too many goals at the beginning of a new year, only to fall back in the same old ruts as they became too overwhelming.

Teresa helped me break down my goals into small, doable Projects. Through the REALIFE Process, I was able to discover the power of focusing on just a few Projects for a short period of time, rather than trying to change everything in my life at once.

I love how the REALIFE Process starts with self-discovery. By learning what I need and value, I was able to find clarity on what is most important to me, which showed me what to do and how to focus my time.

What makes this process different from typical goal-setting systems is that it focuses on your whole life and self, not just work and productivity. It includes the people in your life, your physical and spiritual health, and even making time to have fun.

By looking at my life as a whole, rather than only focusing on what I can achieve, it elevated the importance of growing in EVERY area of my life.

—Lindsay Sterchi, Marketing Director for the REALIFE Process®

The Gift of Intentionality

As you can see, taking these intentional steps to address key Areas of Focus with Action Steps can lead to some wonderful life rewards. In fact, what I and my team have found—as have many of our coaches and clients—is that being intentional in these 90 days has led to creating a habit of action! It has become a behavior and a routine that is not only effective but life-giving as well.

Chris Heinz, a *REALIFE Process Certified Facilitator*, shares just how this kind of intentional approach has helped him in key areas of his life and work.

> I can't imagine where I or my work would be without the REALIFE Process. It has helped me to prioritize my Projects, gain control over my time, and say no to work that doesn't need to get done. What's more, it has delivered peace and confidence to me. Instead of feeling controlled by my to-do list, I now feel in control of my to-do list. My work now works for me.
>
> By choosing three Projects for the quarter, I can complete Action Steps that help me complete the Projects. What once seemed impossible when I looked at the Projects all at once, now seems possible because they're broken down into bite-sized Action Steps. I don't feel anxious or over-

> whelmed anymore.
>
> Now I look forward to planning the upcoming quarter because I know the work will be manageable, purposeful, and intentional. I'm grateful for the freedom and power the REALIFE Process has delivered to me!

That's what creating a *Modern Day Rule of Life* is all about! When viewed and executed in this way, it allows the things in your life that matter to rise to the top. Whether it's relationships, spiritual growth, work, or your health—it is all worth pursuing. It's just having a process for how and when.

And as you can see, it is possible to make small changes that help usher in new rhythms, behaviors, routines, and a calm to your life that is sustainable for the long term. Living from rest, not rush is the desire of our hearts.

Next, we are going to take a look at Component Three in the REALIFE Process and explore how we find REALIFE Time™ so that we can have forward motion in our everyday, ordinary life through the framework of our daily calendar.

CREATE IMPACT

CHAPTER 6:

REALIFE Time™ – Component Three

"It was a long weary time, for the Boy was too ill to play, and the little Rabbit found it rather dull with nothing to do all day long. But he snuggled down patiently, and looked forward to the time when the Boy should be well again, and they would go out in the garden amongst the flowers and the butterflies and play splendid games in the raspberry thicket like they used to."

—Margery Williams, *The Velveteen Rabbit*

I had always been addicted to managing my time well. Unfortunately, my old way of managing time came more from a place of productivity and the need to just get things done—to be able to check things efficiently off my to-do list. But in those years of learning about myself and how to "be" first before "doing" anything, I had begun to do a fair amount of work around managing my time in a healthier way.

When Eric passed away though, I realized that I still had a lot of discovery and awareness to do around this area of time. In fact, it was during Eric's funeral that the need to manage my time in a healthier way was brought home to me in a very poignant way.

Over 600 people attended Eric's funeral that Sunday afternoon in August of 2017, including friends that I hadn't really seen much since high school. In fact, there had been four of us during those high school days that had become close and had continued that friendship far into our adult years. One of those high school friends later became my sister-in-law, which was a special gift to me.

Over the years, my three friends had worked really hard to stay connected; even when my sister-in-law later moved to Montana, they all still got together. Often they would fly to see one another, but just as often, it seemed I always had other things to do, work to attend to, lists to complete. I never could find the time because I was always giving whatever job I had at the time all my attention.

That day when I saw them at the funeral, it became very obvious to me that these friends were close. In fact, it hit me like a ton of bricks that day just how much I had been missing out on by not making the time to spend with these friends. These relationships mattered to me, and yet I was not giving them the attention they deserved. Instead, I was giving my time to work, and in turn, the people in my life, relationships that I said mattered, were only getting the leftover pieces of me. I looked around the church that day and saw many people that mattered to me, and yet they were nowhere to be found on my calendar.

It was time to change that in my life. It was time to live differently knowing that these are the things that truly matter. That's why this particular component of REALIFE Time™ matters because through the process we have been creating, the way we choose to manage our time can lead us to regret missing moments that mattered or regret not savoring them.

REALIFE in Real Life

Time is a precious gift, and I long to steward it well, and the REALIFE Process helps me do that. I recognize time as a gift in many moments of life, but the most impactful are times of intense pain and pure joy. The time recognizers in my life of pain came through the loss of a loved one, the loss of a good friend, and during a season of career transition. It also came through those pure, joyful moments where I savored special moments of time with my family and my friends, having great conversations and spending quality time with my Lord Jesus Christ.

Personally, the TIME Blocks in the REALIFE Process represent the areas of life that matter most to my heart. I see them as an opportunity to release my ways and embrace God's ways, to receive God's love and to give God's love. With God through prayer, he transforms all these blocks into prayer-powered blocks of time that allow me to be more generous with my time. It also allows me to move through life with a peaceful, prayerful productivity, allowing me to invest in my relationship with God, invest in the people around me, and invest the business I love to do.

Now as a REALIFE Process® Certified Facilitator, I too, like Teresa, can hopefully echo God's heart out into the world.

—Michelle Mullins, REALIFE Process Certified Facilitator

Creating a Framework

As we explore Component Three in the REALIFE Process, it is this idea that REALIFE Time™ is really about creating a framework around your day-to-day calendar so that each day matters, and in the end, becomes an extraordinary day. Why an extraordinary day? Why not just a regular or ordinary day? Well, in the spring of 2018, about six months after we lost Eric, I was beginning to share on the Facebook platform about different things happening in my life. Around that same time, we were beginning to celebrate the season of Lent, and I had started a small but new practice of pausing and finding one thing that was extraordinary about that day. The idea was to stop and pause and simply be present in that moment.

As I did this, I started posting my small but extraordinary moments on Facebook. I simply listed the day and the number of the picture and titled it "Ordinary and Extraordinary." The point was to notice something out of your ordinary day and find the extraordinary moment in it. I believe every day has one if we just look for it. What started as one photo has now become a daily spiritual practice for me and has been going for over 1,400 days in a row now. That's almost four years' worth of photos. One for every single day in the year.

Every ordinary day has an extraordinary moment:
we just have to look for them.

Why do I bring that up now? At the beginning of this "time" chapter? Because I realized that it helped me look at time differently throughout the day, and maybe it will help you too. Looking for the moments that are extraordinary helps me slow down in my day. It helps me to look for margin or white space in my calendar to pause. It makes me notice God's presence throughout the day instead of just rushing around like my hair is on fire.

Instead of asking, "What do I need to get done today?" I find myself having a different kind of conversation. Instead I look at the environment around me and nature. I look at relationships. I look at my quiet time and ask God to show me where He is showing up so that I might be present in that moment as well.

Every ordinary day has its own extraordinary moments; we just have to look for them. It is a beautiful practice in and of itself, but it is a practice that also allows me to think about my day through a vastly different lens than before. A lens that helps me form a framework from a place of being and not just doing.

I invite you to do the same. Remember the worksheets for this component of the process can be found on the resource page online at therealifeprocess.com/bookresources.

REALIFE in Real Life

The REALIFE Process gives me the language, framework, and structure to feel freer in both my personal life and my coaching practice. I found my heart beating strongly and more empowered to use the gift of time intentionally and with focus and allow God to multiply it for me.

I now see that, although time creates the "doing" part, it's tied back to my "being" through the REALIFE Process. Thus, I have a much better sense of my being, so what I do is directed in alignment to who God created me to become.

—Nancy Lopez, REALIFE Process Certified Facilitator

REALIFE TIME Blocks™

Here at the REALIFE Process, we like to give language around four key REALIFE TIME Blocks™ on your calendar. Why these four? Because often when I start to work with a client and I start helping them to identify the things that are filling up their day, we find the things they are doing really need to fall into one of these four key blocks or they may not belong on their calendar.

Sometimes, in fact, the best way I can help our clients is by helping them to reframe how they are seeing and looking at their days. Often a client will come to me and say, "I am so busy!" and yet not feel as if they are accomplishing anything or that key areas of their life are not reflected in their calendar.

And yet when I began to ask them to recount their day to me, they say things like: "Oh, I went to the gym today and then grabbed coffee with a friend." To which I reply, "When you went to the gym, that was practicing self-care. When you went and had coffee with your friend, that was actually pouring into someone that matters to you." In that moment, the reframe of how they are seeing their everyday, ordinary calendar shows them that they may be living out more of those things that matter to them than they first thought.

By giving specific language around these four REALIFE TIME Blocks, we can help people reframe what is already in their calendars and make sure it aligns with their Areas of Focus and their Needs and Values. This alignment helps us to get the things that really matter to them on their calendar.

I encourage our clients, just as I encourage you, our reader, to work with your current calendar and begin to build it out based on the REALIFE calendar in your downloadable resources and what you desire to have going forward. Ask yourself these questions: "How do I want to order and align my days, just like it says in Romans 12:1 (MSG)?" and "How can I truly be present to the day and show up as the truest version of myself so my needs and my values are reflected within the framework of my calendar?"

At the REALIFE Process, we look at time in this way: PRESENT Blocks, PEOPLE Blocks, PROJECT Blocks, and PREP

Blocks. There is a reason we look at the blocks in this order and begin to fill in the blanks in this way. To do that, we start with the first block.

PRESENT Blocks™

The PRESENT Block™ asks the question, "How am I going to become present to my own self-care and soul-care?" Remember that the PRESENT Block is a specific and daily block of time for self-care and soul-care. For example, a working mom or young mom may only be able to add a PRESENT Block of 10 minutes to her calendar three days a week.

While I encourage this block to be daily, I realize that different seasons of life allow for greater flexibility than other seasons.

If possible, I also recommend you schedule a half-day PRESENT Block once a month. During this half-day block of time, work to be present to your own self-care. This might mean going on a hike, going for a long run, playing a round of golf, getting your nails done, or even getting a massage. Maybe it's taking time to sit down and read a good book. Focus on whatever helps you care for yourself and take care of your soul.

Then, once a quarter, we encourage you to take a whole day or maybe a whole weekend to just be present to yourself. We believe this is God's invitation to come away with Him and take time for personal growth, rest, and renewal.

PEOPLE Blocks™

At the beginning of this chapter, I shared my realization that I needed to be giving more time to the relationships in my life that mattered to me. When I started working with my own calendar, I realized that the thing that was missing from my allotted time was people.

Often, when I go to conferences to speak or lead a workshop, and I ask the attendees to look at their calendar, most of the time the block that is most glaringly missing is people. This is why I encourage you to add three to four 60–90 minute time blocks in your calendar to give attention to those relationships. Not sure where to start or who to add first? I encourage you to grab a piece of paper and start making a list of family members, friends, colleagues, people in your community, a mentor or a coach.

While you can't meet up with everyone at once, you can begin to add a few to your calendar for each 90-day block and start working on those relationships. After 90 days, move on to the next folks on your list. In a year's time, you will be surprised at how many folks you will have begun to strengthen relationships with. Using the PEOPLE Block™ worksheet provided in your resources will be extremely helpful in this process as well as talking through this with a facilitator or coach.

In the same way, take time to look at the list of people and add those whom you need to STOP giving time to on your calendar—people that are not life-giving to you or a positive influence on your life.

I would encourage you to hold the space in the calendar even if you don't know who will go into a PEOPLE Block time block yet. God will provide the right person for that time, and you will love the feeling of being fully present to that person because you chose to set aside the time.

Before we move on to the third block, let me just say that by addressing the PRESENT and PEOPLE Blocks first, it's like putting on your own oxygen mask first before you help other people. Prioritize self- and soul-care followed by taking care of those whom you have identified as most important.

When I go out and do workshops on time management, no one ever says, "Man, I wish I worked more!" In fact, most people say they wish they had more time with family and the people that matter to them in their life.

PROJECT Blocks™

In this third block, you will want to identify time in your calendar to work on those Projects you identified in Component Two, REALIFE Action. Maybe one of your Projects for the next 90 days is to work on your health. Now you have to decide where you can block out time to work at the Action Steps around that specific area of health focus.

According to Cal Newport, in his book *Deep Work*, it is important to try to get about an hour to an hour and a half of time so that you can really focus enough time on moving your Projects forward. Keep in mind that these PROJECT Blocks™ still have to fit around your everyday, ordinary life. If you work a 9–5 job, then you will need to block that time for your job along with blocking time for your Projects.

If a Project is something like cleaning out your garage, then it might be easier to set aside a block of time for that Project over several Saturdays versus blocking short 30-minute time blocks like you would to call the doctor and schedule that important health appointment. Ideally you will be able to schedule two to four PROJECT Blocks a week where you can do this deeper Project work. Remember to pay attention to how these Projects align with your Needs and Values.

So why are the time blocks important? By predeciding some of these key time blocks, and even having some of them reoccurring, we keep our brains from becoming exhausted and overwhelmed with decision-making, which can sometimes lead to decision fatigue.

According to Jonathan Levav, a professor at Stanford University who studies behavioral decision theory, "If you make a lot of decisions repeatedly, that has an effect on subsequent decisions. As people make more decisions, they're more likely to simplify whatever subsequent decisions they're dealing with."[1] I often say this is why we choose ice cream instead of vegetables as a late-night snack. Our brain is done making decisions! At least the good ones.

Because you have already decided what your calendar will look like, then your days can begin to flow more authentically to who you are, and you will feel less pulled from the doing side of your nature.

PREP Blocks™

PREP Blocks™ are important to the flow of our days, and yet with PREP Blocks, we need to make sure we have boundaries around them so they don't run off with our day. For most people that I work with at the REALIFE Process, I find that they tend to spend the majority of their time doing *Tasks. Tasks* are different from Action Steps because Action Steps pertain to our Projects and Tasks are the "to-do" of our day.

However, we all have everyday, ordinary Tasks that we all must deal with during our normal day-to-day lives, such as answering the phone, responding to emails, or running errands. Often we call it our to-do list or those natural interruptions that can occur in our day.

That is why I talked about the need for margin, or white space, in your calendar as well because there is no way to always predict the

---

1 Shai Danziger, Jonathan Levav and Liora Avnaim-Pesso, "Extraneous Factors in Judicial Decisions," *Proceedings of the National Academy of Sciences*, 108/17 (2011), 6889–92, https://www.pnas.org/content/108/17/6889.

interruptions that will come into any part of your day. However, by having PREP Blocks and white space mapped out in our calendar, we can navigate those tasks and interruptions in a much healthier manner without allowing them to overrun our lives. Remember the headspace needed when we put the pickles in the jar? The same is true of our calendar. It needs margin or white space.

Many people naturally want to start with the PREP Block, but we have to realize that time management is also about putting boundaries on certain aspects of our calendars, specifically as it relates to task management. For example, blocking off 30–45 minutes in the morning to take care of quick to-do tasks, following your PRESENT Block but before you dive into your PROJECT Block or other deep work, will help you meet those task needs and still keep healthy boundaries around your calendar. Decide that you are not going to live out of your inbox as so many people tend or default to do.

In fact, using these shorter PREP Blocks to add margin to your day is another great use of your time. Reflecting back on my earlier pickle jar illustration, if the pickle jar reflects your calendar and the juice is all the tasks in your day, if you only fill the jar with pickle juice and then try to fit the pickles in, you end up spilling juice everywhere and are not able to fit anything else in. In the same way, by leaving a little bit of white space at the top of the pickle jar, we can allow for those unexpected things to happen without causing the jar to overflow.

In fact, during the day-to-day management of my calendar, if I have an appointment canceled, I make sure I am not filling it up automatically with something else. It's easy to do, but by allowing that white space to remain, I actually open up additional time for self- and/or soul-care.

REALIFE in Real Life

The REALIFE Process has given me permission to let go of all the dozens of things that made me busy and unproductive and focus on the most important people and projects with much greater intention.

For example, for a few years, I had drifted away from a lot of people in my life, most notably my five sisters. I filled my days with so much busywork, projects, and commitments that I had drifted away from the important people in my life. When I shifted to focusing more time and attention on deepening my relationships with my sisters, our relationships became deep and beautiful.

When it came to productivity, before the REALIFE Process, I had spent years juggling dozens of projects at a time. Naturally, I'd get stuck managing way too many half-done projects and hardly anything would get done. Implementing the whole concept of focusing on just 90 days at a time changed all of that for me. It shifted my energy and attention on one or two Projects during rolling 90-day time periods. That's caused me to accomplish much more than I had ever been able to when I was trying to do 50 things at once.

I'm so grateful for the REALIFE Process and how it's helped me be more creative, productive, and impactful than ever.

—Susan K. Jones, REALIFE Process Certified Facilitator

Maggie Meylor, a REALIFE client, shares this about her experience with the REALIFE Process:

> I have seen the benefits of following the REALIFE Process and experienced how it removes the anxiety in your life

> by creating a process where you can make decisions and establish your best REALIFE. It gives you confidence in how you can make decisions and establish your calendar. I mean, so many of our calendars create anxiety because we don't have margins or we overbook ourselves. The REALIFE Process gives you the tools to create the life you want to live and be in relationship with the people you want to be in relationship with.

Colleen, another one of our REALIFE clients, expresses how the REALIFE Process has helped her actually find more time.

> The REALIFE Process and utilizing the time blocks has helped me tremendously because I was able to find a day and a half of time. That has really helped me in every aspect of my life. I have more time to relax or more time to do work if I want to. I actually time block every week because my week changes so rapidly. But each week, there's always that extra day and a half where I can schedule different things. And it's wonderful, because now I feel like I can get everything done that I need to.

I encourage you to capture what you've discovered in the framework of your calendar, either digitally or on paper, but be consistent over the next 90 days to use the same tool. I also encourage you as you walk through the FREE downloadable worksheets for the fourth component that you write down what you have learned about yourself through the four REALIFE TIME Blocks. Write down what you've learned on your REALIFE VIEW Document.

Section 6: How Will I Spend My PRESENT Block Time in the Next 90 Days?

Section 7: Who Are the Important People in My PEOPLE Blocks in the Next 90 Days?

By writing these things down in a specific place, we continue to add to our new *Modern Day Rule of Life*—our map that we will reference and follow.

Learning to think of your calendar as a framework that you get to build from is such a freeing concept for so many of our clients who work through the process. By always coming back to the tools you used at the beginning of the process like your REALIFE Needs and Values Assessment, what you've learned about your personality, your Areas of Focus, and then walking out your everyday, ordinary life—your eating, sleeping, going-to-work life—brings joy and wonder to the days you have before you. My good friend Dan Miller often says the phrase "What does this make possible?" When our days align with who we are from the inside out, the possibilities are endless.

“HAVING MARGIN IN YOUR DAY GIVES SPACE FOR MEMORIES TO BE CREATED.”

CHAPTER 7:

REALIFE Living™ – Component Four

"If you don't come apart for a while, you will come apart after a while."

—Dallas Willard

As a child, I grew up in a loving home that was full of life and hard work. My dad was a farmer and my mom was a teacher, which meant that times of rest in our family were few and far between. Both of my parents worked extremely hard in their chosen professions. My mom, being an English teacher, would often stay up late grading papers at the table after a long day in the classroom.

In fact, my mom didn't actually become a teacher until later in my childhood and went back to school for her teaching license while I was still in kindergarten. Some of my earliest memories are of Mom sitting at the table, late in the evening, diligently working on her homework as she pursued her teaching degree.

However, despite working on her degree, caring for our home, and later actively teaching, she was always present to me and my brother, never missing even one of my brother's ball games or other activities in our young lives.

As a farmer, there were various times throughout the year, mostly around planting and harvesting season, when my dad spent long days in the field. I recall, as a child, feeling like there were times I did not see him for a week or two during the busiest times on the farm. I am confident he was present, but as a young child, I didn't always perceive his daily presence because of the heavy workload he carried.

Growing up as we did, my brother and I learned a strong work ethic from our earliest days. I can remember helping my dad pull weeds and cut corn out of the beans, and tagging along early in the morning as Dad checked the fields before the heat of the day set in.

Saturdays were always chore days, filled with cleaning the house, mowing the yard, and weeding the garden. As a child, this kind of hard work ethic developed and nurtured the part of my personality that was quick to take initiative and taught me to always think of the next things that needed to be done.

Being raised in a strong Christian home, Sundays were deemed a day of worship, which meant church attendance both morning and evening. There was always this unspoken expectation that we were to be present when the doors of the church building were open. While technically a day of rest, as a child Sundays always felt like another day of work, and later as a teen and young adult, that could feel like a burden.

Living at a distance from church as we did, we would drive home from the morning service, eat a big Sunday lunch, which was fixed by my mom every single week. Following lunch, we had a few hours to ourselves before returning to the church for the evening service.

When the middle and high school years came along, it seemed like there was always somebody coming over for the Sunday meal, which meant we were now entertaining friends and church family on a regular basis. Rarely did it feel restful, and many times the day felt very rushed.

Later in life, as I wrestled with defining what a sustainable life actually looked like for me, I found it very difficult to figure out how to live from a place of rest and peace. It felt very foreign to me because I had never really seen it modeled, and I certainly had never practiced it.

My college years were not much different from middle and high school. During my college years, I often worked on Sundays to catch up on my schoolwork or at a part-time job, though even then my time was short and jammed packed with activities outside of homework. As a member of my college choir, I frequently spent Sundays traveling with the group to do concerts, often arriving home late for classes the next day.

In my adult years, in particular during the 15 years of ministry work, it only served to emphasize the work rhythm that Sunday had become for me. As a worship pastor, Sundays were just another workday that repeated itself in a frantic cycle every seven days. Sabbath, while a great idea in theory, was not something I really understood or knew how to practice in that season of my life.

It wasn't until I came to the Transforming Center that I began the process of really understanding and desiring to practice a Sabbath day of rest. It was with this new understanding that this concept of a work and rest rhythm began to really shift in my life. I started asking the question, "What would it feel like to slow my body, mind, and heart to a quieter place of rest and not always a place of rush?"

I knew that I needed it and, surprisingly, realized I actually craved it. Have you ever craved rest? Craved the slowness and the simplicity that rest can bring? It is a strange but wonderful sense that something so simple could have such a profound effect on our lives.

My old work compass would have said that resting meant no cooking, no mowing the lawn, or anything that resembled work of any sort. And yet, I realized that defining what rest looked like was ultimately up to me. I had to throw out the old compass and find a new bearing to figure out what life-giving rest really looked like for me.

This defining of *Rest* and its closely related companions—*Renew* & *Review*—is what has helped me create this fourth component of the REALIFE Process. This is truly the key to creating a sustainable *Modern Day Rule of Life*. I realize now that the Rest, Renew, and Review component was the missing part of so many of the self-help models I had tried before. Those models talked about managing behaviors, habits, and time but failed to mention that God also designed us for rest. As humans, we are created in God's image, and we often forget that God rested. Resting is a part of farm life I have come to know well. Rest is what keeps the ground sustainable and allows it to prosper when it's time for planting again. We are the same way. If we want to live a sustainable God-honoring life that we can prosper in, we must learn how to do so from a place of rest.

"Ruthlessly eliminate hurry from your life."

—Dallas Willard

Rest and Renew

Rest is defined as the act of ceasing "work or movement in order to relax, refresh oneself, or recover strength." (Encyclopedia.com) In similar ways, renew is defined as a way "to make like new

: restore to freshness, vigor, or perfection." However, I know that we can find this idea of Rest and Renewal so very hard to carry out.

During my time at the Transforming Center, encouraged to reflect on my childhood, I realized that despite the busyness of our family life, I had found ways to rest and renew as a child. Often this rest and renewal came through writing music, hours spent playing in the woods, and going for long horseback rides. I see now that these activities from my childhood played a vital role in helping me rest and renew and even how I understand rest and renewal today.

I vividly remember that when I was in fourth grade, my parents gave me an autoharp for Christmas. I had always loved playing the piano, and now I could add the autoharp to that list of things I loved. That gift opened up the world of music to me even more. To this day, writing and playing music is a key way I connect with God and allow Him to renew my body, mind, and spirit.

As a child, I loved long walks on my own and relished long hours in the woods to just play and explore. Even though people today see me as a forward-moving and extroverted person, truth be told, I love to be by myself and soak in those quiet moments of reflection, rest, and renewal as well. Sometimes this means going for long drives in my little red Miata convertible, sitting on the porch with friends, grabbing a good cup of coffee at the local coffee shop, or simply working in my wildflower garden. In a lot of ways, returning to my childhood patterns of rest and renewal was simply about remembering.

My spiritual director, Sibyl Towner, talks about the word "remember," saying that "to remember is to go back and put something back together, to make it whole again." I have had to go back to those early years and remember what brought me life and then find ways to reintroduce them into the rhythms of my everyday life.

So how do we take the necessary steps to rest and renew? How do we put practical action to this idea of Resting and Renewing on a regular basis? It all comes down to the process of *Reviewing*.

Review

In 2011, when I started working with my then mentor Rory Noland, he began to teach me the process of Reviewing. As a forward-moving type, I had a tendency to always be looking forward and never taking a pause long enough to process what was behind.

I rarely, if ever, left a season or situation in my life that I took time to pause and ask myself: "How did that experience or season feel for me?" or "What do I want to take away from that? What do I want to learn? What am I grateful for?"

I never thought to pause because I was always so busy moving and looking ahead. However, by not pausing, I was not allowing my body, heart, and mind the space they needed to transition to a new season or into a new experience. I simply kept running through life with my hair on fire. It wasn't until Rory challenged me to actually pause that I started learning the value of sitting quietly and of resting and allowing my spirit to be renewed. I found it very hard at first to sit there and do absolutely nothing. How does one do that when you're so used to living with your hair on fire?

But that first step of sitting quietly for five minutes was a building block toward learning to Review—of learning to sit in the quiet, to let God speak to my heart and mind as I spent time Reviewing my life. Later, as Rory invited me to become a part of the Transforming Center, I found myself getting away once a quarter to Review and Rest, which in turn was so Renewing. Over time, the rhythm of getting away has become a spiritual practice for me, allowing me to look back but also giving me new energy to look forward.

Today I spend 30–45 minutes at the beginning of each week Reviewing. I Review what is behind me and what is in front of me but notice where I want to be present. This weekly practice has become integral to remaining balanced and not returning to a life living from rush.

Sustainability

So how do we bring these three important components together—Rest, Renew, and Review—and make them actually sustainable.

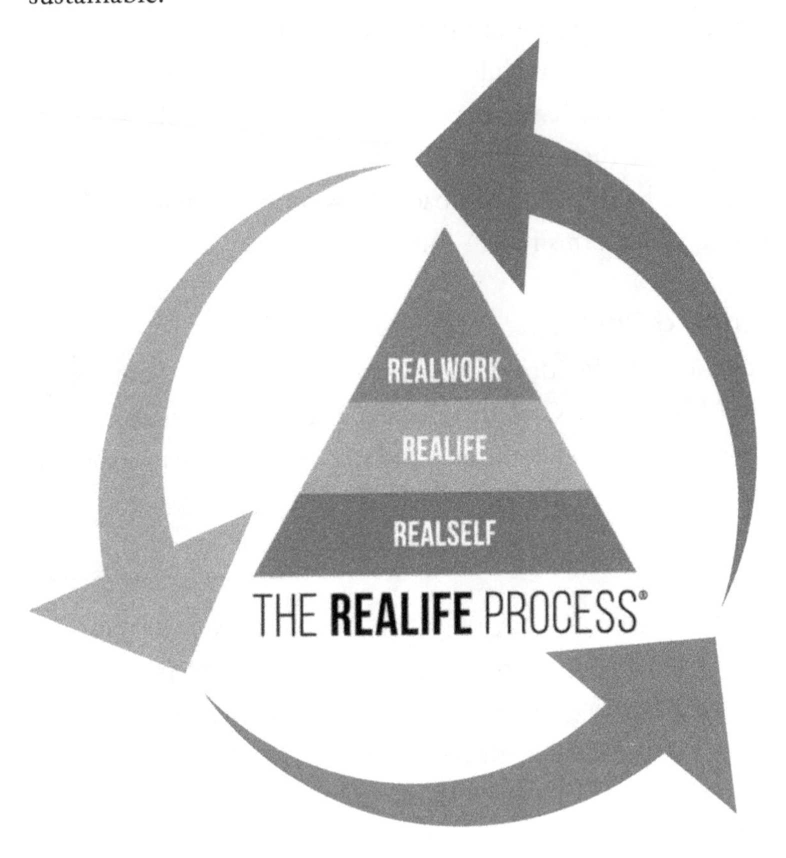

When I am working with clients or any of our *REALIFE Process Certified Facilitators*, I share the above graphic, showing how the arrows encircle our REALSELF, our REALIFE, and our REALWORK. These arrows represent this fourth component of Rest, Renew, and Review.

When these three things are flowing full circle in our life through appropriate behaviors, rhythms, and routines, there is sustainable energy that is given into our REALSELF, REALIFE, and REALWORK.

I love this quote from Dallas Willard, who says this about the importance of stepping away and finding rest and renewal: "If you don't come apart for a while, you will come apart after a while." Indeed, truer words have never been spoken. So let's take a look at how to practice these in more detail.

(Again, the FREE downloadable worksheets will also help walk you through this fourth component.)

Practicing Resting

Let's look at the idea of *Rest* first. When we talk about rest at the REALIFE Process, we are referring to a choice we make to step back and rest our bodies, minds, and spirits. There are two specific ways we challenge you to step back and rest.

"Most of us are more tired than we know at the soul level. We are teetering on the brink of dangerous exhaustion, and we cannot do anything else until we have gotten some rest ... we can't really engage [any spiritual disciplines] until solitude becomes a place of rest for us rather than another place for human striving and hard work."

–Ruth Haley Barton, *Sacred Rhythms: Arranging Our Lives for Spiritual Transformation*

Weekly Rest

The first step toward getting the rest you need is setting aside a weekly time of intentional rest.

For me, this weekly rest is an intentional 10- to 12-hour window of time that I step back from technology and work and purposefully slow my life down as Richard Rohr says, "to two miles an hour." In this slowed-down state, I take time to notice the little things around me such as nature and its beauty. I practice being present to the people in my world whom I love and care about, and I spend time with God through reading and worship.

This intentional stepping back is a practice we encourage you to build into the framework of your calendar every single week. Initially, it might feel difficult or strange, but don't become discouraged because the more you practice this type of rest, the more it will begin to impact your day-to-day life in extraordinary ways.

Some of our clients and facilitators choose to call this intentional day of rest, Sabbath, but whatever you call it, know that it is important to the renewing part of your being. It is the introduction of this practice that will allow you to start stepping out of the drivenness of your work, career, or life calling, and also, maybe a little bit out of your ordinary life.

Quarterly Rest

The second way we step back and rest is by intentionally stepping away every 90 days for 24–48 hours. This longer block of time is where you are shutting down for a few days to really rest and be present to your body, mind, and your heart. This quarterly rest might be incorporated as part of your 90 DAY Reset that we will talk about in chapter 9.

Getting into this weekly and quarterly routine of rest is what helps make life sustainable.

REALIFE in Real Life

The REALIFE Process is a truly unique framework for bringing order, purpose, and focus into the life of anyone seeking structure and inspiration. Teresa McCloy and the REALIFE team have crafted practical tools for shaping our God-given design, values, and priorities into fulfilling projects, with specific actions and realistic timelines

From the REALIFE VIEW to REALIFE Living, the entire process protects me from slipping back into living with my hair on fire. The 90 DAY Reset provides the guard rails I need to periodically slow down and cultivate the sacred, life-giving rhythms of Rest and Renewal that support my discernment of what needs to be planted, pruned, and tended in my life, work, and relationships.

Teresa, her team, and her REALIFE Process can help anyone looking to do more of what matters and steward ordinary, everyday lives into extraordinary legacies!

—Natalie Guzman, REALIFE Process Certified Facilitator

Practicing Renewing

Now, let's look at the *Renewing* piece of a sustainable life. At the REALIFE Process, we look at renewing as engaging your mind, body, and soul in different ways than your normal day-to-day rhythm. For instance, if you work at a computer all day, taking time to put your body in motion by taking a walk in nature serves to renew your mind, body, and soul.

Renewing is best done by engaging in things you like to do and/or things that you find relaxing such as running, hiking, or gardening. If you always read self-help or entrepreneurial books, maybe try picking up a novel or reading an inspirational piece in order to engage your brain in a different way. This is where your hobbies and fun activities fit into your calendar. Many times this actually shows up as a PRESENT Block on your calendar. You can see how the process weaves together to form behaviors, rhythms, and routines. It all belongs together.

I encourage you to take a half- to a full-day pause, if possible, for the Renewal piece of the process. For some, Saturday becomes their Renewal day and Sunday (or Sabbath) becomes their Rest day.

This is how Renewal fleshes out in my own life. Friday evening is usually spent as a PEOPLE Block that includes a date night with my husband, Dale. Saturday is a day of Renewal, often spent with family or pursuing a favorite hobby and ending with dinner at home as we prepare for Sabbath and Rest on the next day. Sunday includes worship in the morning with our church family, followed by lunch and sometimes a nap or something very low-key with friends. By evening time, I am moving into the third piece of a sustainable life: Review.

Practicing Reviewing

While it is the last step in our rhythm and routines, *Review* is the most vital step in leading a sustainable life and an important pause before diving into any new week or a new quarter.

Weekly Review

My time of Review happens once a week on Sunday evening. After a few days of Renewing and Rest, I am ready to review my past week as well as the one in front of me. It takes 35–45 minutes. I am looking back at the last week or 10 days, noting where I am at with certain Projects and also looking at the framework of my calendar. I ask myself several key questions: "What is coming up in the next couple of weeks? What do I need to finish or where do I need to tie up Action Steps in order to bring that Project into a new week?"

I also spend time reconnecting with my REALIFE VIEW Document—a two-page document—where, on the first page, I have captured in writing who I am being, and on the second page, I have captured what I am currently pursuing. I am reflecting on the next 90 days, the people I have committed to connect with, and how I am choosing to be present in my life.

There is something powerful about reviewing your REALIFE VIEW Document every week. It literally only takes about five minutes to read through what you have captured, but it is such an important part of your weekly Review.

Often I find that when I have had a particularly hard week or life feels off track, it is good to remember who I am, whose I am, what really matters to me, and how I have been created and designed uniquely by God. This short window of Review gets me back on track and focused on my Projects and how I am choosing to move forward in my life. It also reminds me that I am choosing to live my life from rest and not from rush, which is vital to living authentically into the *Modern Day Rule of Life* that I have designed for myself.

Quarterly Review

This short, but important Review, happens every week but then also every 90 days. When I step away to rest for 24–48 hours, I am able to get up on the balcony of my life and take time to Review as well. Now, keep in mind that this review time is not about recreating your rule of life, but instead it is a chance to look at each area of your life from a 30,000-foot view and ask, "Is this still true for me and what really matters in my life? Are these the Projects I still want to be focused on for the next few months, or are they complete and I need to look at the Areas of Focus again and choose new Projects? Is there anything that doesn't feel authentic to life right now?"

Depending on how you answer those questions, you then have the opportunity to make changes to your REALIFE VIEW Document and continue to craft your life, your way. Remember, these are tools to simply help you craft YOUR life, in a way that uniquely fits you.

I love the perspective that Winston Faircloth—one of our *REALIFE Process Certified Facilitators* —shared with me recently in regard to this: "It is really easy to drift if we do not live this precious life with intentionality. Instead, we run the risk of waking up 10 years later and wondering where our life has gone without any real movement or change. I'm 60 now and I don't know how many more decades I have, but I want to live the life I have left with even more focus, more presence, and more intentionality. That's why I am thankful for the tools that Teresa and the REALIFE Process have given me, allowing me to live a more intentional life." Is it easy to become intentional? No. It does take a lot of focused work over a length of time. Remember, this process is a marathon, not a sprint. However, with continued focus and practice, we can each live a REALIFE of sustainable rhythms and routines of *Rest, Renew*, and focused *Review.*

“EVERY ORDINARY DAY HAS EXTRAORDINARY MOMENTS; YOU JUST HAVE TO LOOK FOR THEM.”

LIVING FROM REST

CHAPTER 8:
Practices behind the Process

> "Weeks passed, and the little Rabbit grew very old and shabby, but the Boy loved him just as much. He loved him so hard that he loved all his whiskers off, and the pink lining to his ears turned grey, and his brown spots faded. He even began to lose his shape, and he scarcely looked like a rabbit any more, except to the Boy. To him he was always beautiful, and that was all that the little Rabbit cared about. He didn't mind how he looked to other people, because the nursery magic had made him Real, and when you are Real shabbiness doesn't matter."
>
> **—Margery Williams, *The Velveteen Rabbit***

When I first started creating the components of, what is now, the REALIFE Process, I created it out of a need in my own life. I had the need for consistency in my life, a desire to feel grounded and to no longer feel like life was falling apart. Back in 2011, when Eric told us that he was addicted to heroin, I was living with my hair on fire and my own life was full of chaos and confusion. I had no rhythms and routines. I had no spiritual practices. I had behaviors, but they weren't consistent behaviors that were grounding me. They were behaviors that fed my need for control and conflict.

In those days I was living on a lot of adrenaline, a lot of coffee and caffeine, and spending a lot of time seeking the approval of others. I was codependent in unhealthy ways in several relationships and realize now that I was not in a good place. Looking back, I think I believed that I was in a good place, and to others, it appeared as if my life was in a good and stable place as well. But the truth is, it wasn't. Yet I knew that something was not right and I needed to make a change. It was in the midst of this chaotic and out-of-control season that I finally reached out in desperation to do life differently.

I will forever be thankful that the Lord led me to Rory Noland in that season, to have him walk beside me as my spiritual director, mentor, and coach. It was his caring guidance that set me on a new path.

While there was much I did not know in that early season, what I did know is that if I did not do something to change the way I was living, I might not survive. In truth, I realized that it also meant that my marriage or my relationship with my kids might not survive, and in the end, I would risk losing all the things I would say mattered most to me.

It wasn't anyone's fault that I was at that place. It wasn't Dale's or Anneke's fault and most certainly it wasn't Eric's fault. However, Eric's very real battle with addiction became the catalyst that made me sit up and say, "Whoa, something has to change here." I knew that my behaviors, rhythms, and routines had to be different if real and lasting change was going to happen. This wasn't about reading another self-help book but more about seeking out and creating my own pattern of behavior.

When I think of the spiritual practices that are behind the REALIFE Process, they are built deep and wide because, without this connection to these spiritual practices, there would be no sustainability to the process. These practices are the very ones that helped me create new behaviors, rhythms, and routines, and the practices that now allow me to live from a place of rest and not rush.

Those first days, weeks, and months were all about taking the first small steps. Changing up my morning routine with more healthy practices and learning not to stay up until three o'clock in the morning just to get more work done. In fact, I remember a conversation with a fellow church staff member who asked me at a weekly staff meeting, "I got an email from you at two o'clock in the morning! What were you doing up at two o'clock in the morning?" The sad part is that I remember figuring out how to write the emails at two o'clock in the morning but not have them sent until the morning hours. That was just one of many unhealthy types of behaviors I was creating at the time.

Don't Despise Small Beginnings

Once I realized how unhealthy my behaviors had become, I started with small, incremental steps. Change didn't happen overnight, but every two or three months I would add another small step, and with time, those small steps began to help me create a new *Modern Day Rule of Life* for myself.

Over the years of developing the REALIFE Process, I have learned that many of these new rhythms, behaviors, and routines come in daily cycles and through direct questions we ask of ourselves such as

> What do I want my morning routine to look like? What do I want my evening routine to look like? When do I want to start and end my day?

The last question is especially important if you find yourself in the entrepreneurial space. Most entrepreneurs I know do not work a typical 9–5 routine. It is easy to become out of balance in this area of our life.

You also might ask yourself: "When do I want to start and/or stop using technology in my day? When do I want to hang out with friends? Where does a date night with my spouse fit into my weekly schedule?"

There are a hundred questions you can ask yourself as you start making small steps toward creating your own *Modern Day Rule of Life*. However, the important part is to start asking the questions and identifying the routines and rhythms that God has naturally placed in you for this season of your life.

REALIFE in Real Life

One of the benefits of being a part of the process is the community of other like-minded coaches and entrepreneurs who are living out the same rhythms. Having like-minded people to do life with around a framework is something that I needed in my life. Using the four TIME Blocks to lay out my calendar each week and give me language as to why I was choosing to do something not only has benefited me but is now benefiting the clients that I serve through coaching.

—Tom Mabie, REALIFE Process Certified Facilitator

Weekly and 90 Day Rhythms

I can't say enough about the power of the weekly rhythms of Rest, Renewal, and Review when it comes to living a sustainable and authentic life. It is in the consistent, weekly meeting with yourself that the rhythms, practices, and behaviors that you wish to implement in your life really take hold.

It's important for you to decide where your day of Rest and Renewal will land in your week and how you can best learn to lean into that routine. Those days of Rest and Renewal will be key to supporting your unique needs and values. The practice of Reviewing will allow you to gauge if you are living out of your own authentic self while still leaving space to allow God to meet your needs and connect to your values.

In the same way, it is important to schedule intentional time for a 90 DAY Reset. This may be a time you get away to a favorite place or retreat area so that you lessen the distractions that could derail this important time. If getting away is not always an option, looking around your home and setting aside a space that allows you to step away could be a good solution. Many times, in setting new behaviors, rhythms, and routines, the familiar setting of home is helpful.

The Practice of the Rule of Life

One of the books that has been so significant for me on this journey and in my quiet time, is one I reference often when working with clients and our *REALIFE Process Certified Facilitators*: the *Spiritual Disciplines Handbook* by Adele Calhoun. My personal copy is covered in highlighter, sticky notes, and my own scribbles in the margin.

One of the first practices Adele Calhoun expounds is the practice of the rule of life. It is this rule of life concept that we have built into the REALIFE Process and why we call it a "*Modern Day Rule of Life*," which is our variation on the ancient spiritual practice of the rule of life. It is this defined rule of life that allows us to have guardrails around how we want to show up each and every day.

The Practice of Discernment

Another spiritual practice that we lean heavily on in the REALIFE Process is the practice of discernment. The act of discernment is to recognize God's voice and will for our life. We use discernment in a number of key ways. One of those ways is when we are pre-deciding what are the things that really matter in our life and what we sense and discern God is asking us to focus our time and attention on.

Many times I find my clients are struggling with decision fatigue. It is a very real psychological phenomenon in our culture that happens when we are trying to make too many decisions in a period of time. At times these decisions we are trying to make are really bigger than a decision and need the practice of discernment. As a forward-moving type on the Enneagram, learning to slow down and discern something and listen to God's voice, not just my own ability, was vital for me to learn to live from rest and not rush.

"It's not joy that makes us grateful; it's gratitude that makes us joyful."

—Brené Brown

The Practice of the Examen

The practice of the Examen is sometimes called the Daily Examen and involves reflecting on the events of the day in a prayerful way. This prayerful pause allows us to notice where God's presence has been and pay attention to His direction going forward into a new day. Through the REALIFE Process, we encourage you through the weekly Review to reflect and give this kind of attention. It's the action of looking back to what is past and forward to what is ahead.

It is also a time to honestly ask where we find ourselves with God the most during the week and where we are with Him the least in our week. Did we seek out His presence or did we go on without Him in some way? The purpose of the Examen is to shed light on the rhythms and routines from our week and give an honest assessment of how we actually spent that time. It can also be a time to practice gratitude or use a journal to record things you are grateful for.

The Practice of Solitude and Silence

Silence and solitude are defined by Adele Calhoun in this manner: "Silence is a regenerative practice of attending and listening to God in quiet, without interruption and noise. Silence provides freedom from speaking as well as from listening to words or music. (Reading is also listening to words.)" and "The practice of solitude involves scheduling enough uninterrupted time in a distraction-free environment that you experience isolation and are alone with God. Solitude is a 'container discipline' for the practice of other disciplines."

The active practice of solitude and silence comes during, what we call, PRESENT Blocks in our calendars. It is the time that we set aside for intentional self-care and soul-care. This spiritual practice also comes during times of Renewal, where we have paused from our ordinary day-to-day work and shifted our focus to those things that renew our body, heart, and mind.

Another key area where solitude and silence play a vital part is during times of intentional Rest. Either the weekly time of rest of Sabbath or however you have chosen to add rest to rhythms and routine. Instead of filling your time of rest with noise and distraction, really home in on seeking out solitude and silence. There is something that happens to our very souls when we allow them to experience rest in this quiet but powerful way.

The Practice of Breath Prayer

Breath prayer is a simple practice using the pattern of your breath to breathe deeply while focusing on saying an attribute of God that speaks to you. On the exhale of your breath, focus on sharing the desire of your heart with God. Many people use the same breath prayer for years.

Breath prayer can be practiced all throughout the day to calm yourself and bring you back to a place of slowing and internal rest. Practice simply asking for the desires of God's heart as it relates to your everyday, ordinary life. This practice of breath prayer is also linked to self-care and soul-care, allowing you to pause and slow down as you wait on the Lord.

My breath prayer for years has been, "You are my rock and my redeemer. In you there is hope." I began praying this prayer during times when hope seemed lost. Even to this day, this phrase grounds me back to the moment and brings me present.

These first practices come during and as a part of the practice of Rest in the REALIFE Process.

The Practice of Sabbath

The definition of Sabbath in faith communities is often referred to as a day set aside for rest and worship. As we talked about earlier in the book, Sabbath is a time set aside and defined by you as to what rest looks like, but to practice it well, it does mean this day looks very different from the other days of the week as to what gets done and what does not get done or accomplished. It is a key part of making sure the process will be sustainable throughout your lifetime.

"If we do not allow for a rhythm of rest in our overly busy lives, illness becomes our Sabbath—our pneumonia, our cancer, our heart attack, our accidents create Sabbath for us."

—Wayne Muller, *Sabbath: Finding, Rest, Renewal, and Delight in Our Busy Lives*

The Practice of Retreat

Ruth Haley Barton speaks of retreat in this way: "Retreat in the context of the spiritual life is an extended time apart for the purpose of being with God and giving God our full and undivided attention; it is, as Emilie Griffin puts it, 'a generous commitment to our friendship with God.' The emphasis is on the words extended and generous." Retreating is stepping up to the balcony of your life and taking an overview of the past, present, and future. Sitting with God for an extended period of time around what you are planting, pruning, and tending in your life.

The Practice of Slowing

The practice of slowing is something that you discover throughout the entire process you have been invited to create for yourself. It is a sacred space to take a moment, to see the margin and pauses in your life and notice your breath. The REALIFE Process is built around creating and defining what slowing feels like for you in your own *Modern Day Rule of Life*. It is about living from a sacred place fueled through rest and curbing the addiction to the busyness of a hurried life and the workaholism that we are so easily drawn to. Just breathe!

To learn more about each of these Practices behind the Process, go to our FREE resource page where you can find the podcast episodes where we explore each practice.

"IN ORDER TO LIVE OUT THE PROCESS, YOU WILL NEED TO SUSTAIN THE PRACTICES."

CHAPTER 9:

Practicing a 90 DAY Reset™

"Once you are Real you can't become unreal again. It lasts for always."

—Margery Williams, *The Velveteen Rabbit*

In the fall of 2021, I was preparing to host a retreat for our *REAL-IFE Process Certified Facilitators.* We gather in person twice a year as part of the rhythm we have created in our community. My routine has been to choose a theme for these retreats that builds on our content and also supports our facilitators in the work they are doing in their businesses. As I chose the theme "Abide" for our retreat, it brought me back to one of my favorite scripture passages from John 15:5–8 (NIV).

"I am the vine; you are the branches. If you remain in me and I in you, you will bear much fruit; apart from me you can do nothing. If you do not remain in me, you are like a branch that is thrown away and withers; such branches are picked up, thrown into the fire and burned. If you remain in me and my words remain in you, ask whatever you wish, and it will be done for you. This is to my Father's glory, that you bear much fruit, showing yourselves to be my disciples."

Years ago our daughter had been given this verse to memorize as her weekly Bible verse in the small private school she attended. It had become an important verse in my life over the years, so much so I had even written a worship song referring to this verse.

During this past year, with the pandemic, it seemed a fitting theme for which we were all needing encouragement—leaning into abiding in Him. The invitation from this passage to abide or remain in Him is a constant reminder to me as to where I am rooted and the necessity to pay attention to the trellis and the vines.

As a farm girl, I fully understand the importance of regularly paying attention to what you have planted. Here on the farm, we are constantly monitoring the weather and the temperature, controlling the weeds that are creeping in on the crops and the condition of the soil. As I developed the REALIFE Process, it just seemed natural that I would need to live into a rhythm of abiding and tending to myself on a regular basis.

One of the last pieces of my journey and work in spiritual formation was to write out my own rule of life. And while the rule of life I initially wrote at the Transforming Center back in 2015 was a good start, it was just the beginning. In fact, I realized that in order to remain healthy, I needed to revisit my rule of life on a regular basis.

Crafting a *Modern Day Rule of Life* is similar to building a trellis that is implied to in the John passage. The word "rule" comes from the Latin word "*regula*," which literally means "a straight piece of wood," but it's also the word used for a trellis. So consider what a trellis does for a vine: it supports and provides structure for the vine to grow. Without a trellis, a vine will stop growing, begin to wither, and eventually die.

Our Modern Day Rule of Life gives direction on how to plant, prune, and tend the vine that you are growing and the rule or trellis you are growing on. Without proper pruning or tending, the vine can risk running wild and out of control or even die. In John 15:1–2 (NIV), it reads, "I am the true vine, and my Father is the gardener. He cuts off every branch in me that bears no fruit, while every branch that does bear fruit he prunes so that it will be even more fruitful."

In the same way, a planned time of Review and reset focused around your Modern Day Rule of Life will be vital to growing your vine and keeping you tied to a trellis that is strong and sustainable. My own regular 90 DAY Reset™ helps me continue to live from a place of rest and not rush.

The practice of a 90 DAY Reset™ is just walking back through four key components of the REALIFE Process and reviewing how you are growing. What needs to be planted or replanted, what needs to be pruned, and what needs to be tended or noticed? This part of the process can be completed in several different ways. You may choose to revisit the components of the process one per day over a week's time or you might take an entire day to work through the 90 DAY Reset process.

My favorite way is to spend a 24–48 hour period on retreat and really get back up on the balcony of my life and walk through my REALIFE VIEW Document, rewriting, reflecting, and realigning my life. No matter how you personally dive into the 90 DAY Reset, the important thing is to make it a regular part of the rhythm and routines of your life. Ninety days is not a magical number. However, I find that if we practice the pause about every three months, we can stop the hair-on-fire lifestyle from returning and breathe in again the goodness of whose we truly are. It also allows us to continue the important work of discerning what needs to be planted, pruned, or tended.

Let's look at the four parts of a 90 DAY Reset.

REALIFE in Real Life

Attending the REALIFE Process virtual retreat was such a pivotal time for me. We had just had our second child at the beginning of the pandemic and then moved across the country to be closer to family. We also had a close family member who was walking through a terminal illness, and were helping to care for her children as well as navigating ours. Learning the tool of the Enneagram was so helpful in our marriage as well as the Needs and Values Assessment. During the retreat, I was able to step up on the balcony of my life and see the big picture of all that we were going through and get some perspective. I could see that some of my values were hard to live into when my own needs were not being meant. Silly things like my need to be organized and not having time to unpack from the move were affecting how I was showing up for others. Stepping back and pausing through the retreat and getting a different view was so helpful.

—Kara Janowski, Client

Review Your REALIFE VIEW Document™

In the first part of the 90 DAY Reset, you are going to want to look at your two-page REALIFE VIEW Document. Remember this document is like the compass for your life. It is where you have written your REALIFE Needs and Values and your personal life mission statement. It is where you have identified your Areas of Focus and written your I Am Statement around each of these important areas. Now is the time to decide whether there is anything that you want to rewrite. Maybe something has become clearer in one of these areas in the past 90 days.

The beauty of a 90 DAY Reset is that we have the ability to tweak, hone, and review our Areas of Focus now that we have had a chance to try them on for a little while. This part of the reset I find to be fun because it allows me to really spend time reflecting and discerning my focus on key areas, maybe in my spiritual life, my health, or my career.

Next, spend some time reviewing what your Projects are going to be from these Areas of Focus. What one to three Projects will move you forward in a few of these areas in the next 90 days?

This is where you would want to go back through and use a REALIFE Process Mindmap. Home in on Areas of Focus and Projects, identifying what is needed to keep things moving forward. The temptation will be to create Projects in every Area of Focus. Remember to limit your Projects to just a few so that you create targeted momentum. You will have the opportunity to focus on another area at the next 90 DAY Reset. For example, maybe you have gotten into a great rhythm and routine of exercising, but now you want to focus more specifically on losing weight.

This kind of homed-in review and focus reset allows you to see your accomplishments and how far you have come and allows you to spend time in further discernment about possible next steps. Reviewing and resetting also allows you to spend time in lament for something that didn't move forward or come out as you had anticipated.

Realign Your PRESENT Block Worksheet™

Now that you have reviewed your REALIFE VIEW Document, it's time to realign using your PRESENT Block Worksheet™ again. As you look at your PRESENT Block Worksheet, ask yourself if there are adjustments you need or want to make to your self-care and soul-care? Is there a new rhythm that you want to incorporate such as walking or a book you specifically want to read? Remember, it's important to put on your own oxygen mask first before you can really care well for others.

You might also ask yourself: "How do I want to block that time differently on my calendar? What are some big events happening in the next 90 days that might require me to allow space differently so I can be fully present?"

Ask yourself who you might be able to share those commitments with. Maybe that person is a spouse or a trusted friend, but I find that when I have someone I've shared my commitments with, I am much more likely to see them through.

This is where community becomes so important. Our team members at the REALIFE Process share with each other our 90 DAY Reset commitments, and now that we have the REALIFE Facilitator Network, doing life together around all these things is important to our community.

Angela Gage, a *REALIFE Process Certified Facilitator*, shares just what community has meant for her in this last year, in particular during the height of the 2020 pandemic year: "The greatest challenge has been the emotional challenge of being a sole proprietor. The REALIFE Process Network has encouraged me so much and helped me continue on with my Projects. If it wasn't for the community, I would have probably given up already. Having a community to sit with me and encourage me every week, not every six months, but, you know, every week has really been a lifeline."

Redo Your PEOPLE Block Worksheet™

Using the PEOPLE Block Worksheet™ each 90 days has become the key to strengthening my relationships consistently over the last several years. You will want to redo your PEOPLE Block Worksheet during your reset. As you redo your worksheet, reflect first on the past 90 days and all the people you connected with. Take time to celebrate each one of those people by pausing around their name and giving thanks for them.

Next, tap into the spiritual discipline of discernment and ask yourself, "In these next 90 days, who needs to be present in my life?" I would encourage you to then take time to look at your calendar and block out time so you can reach out to each person and connect with them if needed.

If it's family time you have identified as being important in the next 90 days, you might want to book vacation time together or set up dinner or coffee so you can visit and connect. The key is to reach out now and get it on the calendar in the first week of the new 90 days.

Rewrite Your Next 90 Day Projects

Now it's time to rewrite your new Projects and Action Steps for the next 90 days. Let me encourage you to not rush this part of the process. If you've taken a weekend retreat, then take time to pray over your Projects and even sleep and sit in discernment over them.

This kind of stepping back and sitting quietly is important before just simply diving back in. You'll want to pause again and review your Areas of Focus and decide which areas have a Project in the next 90 days and which areas you are able to maintain. Remember, you can't realistically do more than two to three Projects at a time.

Finally, as time allows, you can ask some other questions such as

- Is there anything I need to reset in my workspace?

- Do I need to clean up anything in my computer or reset how I am relating to technology so that I can really focus?
- Are there any daily habits I've picked up that I want to reset?

One of the things I look at closely during this time is how much my work has crept into my personal time. For example, I always want to protect my morning routine, but over a 90-day period, I can say "yes" to too many early morning meetings due to time zone conflicts and the need to please others. The 90 DAY Reset gives me time to focus on these undesirable habits that have crept in and allows me to not lose important routines in my life.

The Balcony View

It is important to remember that the 90 DAY Reset is not meant to be complicated or a "do-over" of your whole *Modern Day Rule of Life*. Instead, it is taking the resources and tools of the process, stepping up on that balcony, looking back at where you have been, and looking forward toward where you are going. Once you have been able to look it over from those vantage points, then it's time to simply review, realign, redo, and rewrite your REALIFE VIEW Document.

For example, one of the things I have done to hone my own REALIFE VIEW Document is to add scriptures to every one of my Areas of Focus. I have also taken time to connect every one of my REALIFE Needs and Values to my Areas of Focus.

It can be fun, over time, to create and develop your document in deeper and deeper ways. Often these are not the things you would have taken the time for when you first went through the process. However, now you can add additional layers for an even richer experience.

The REALIFE Process is a very personal framework, and each time you do a 90 DAY Reset, you will begin to create your own routines and rhythms. We do have some clients who enjoy the process of rewriting their REALIFE VIEW Document by hand on a fresh worksheet every time. It often helps them process their own REALIFE in a more connected and deeper way. No matter how you choose to work through your 90 DAY Reset, the rhythm of leaning into the process is the most important takeaway from the experience. God will direct the process if you allow the space.

Winston Faircloth, a *REALIFE Process Certified Facilitator*, said this about his experience of walking through a 90 DAY Reset: "Over the past year, I have taken the opportunity to go deep with my 90 DAY Reset and to go through the entire process from beginning to end. In doing so, I have learned that even when it feels like my Needs and Values and my day-to-day are pretty stable, that as I have grown, my Needs and Values also need to become more authentic with me."

REALIFE in Real Life

Who doesn't want or need the opportunity and permission to reset every now and then? I love the 90 DAY Reset because the tool offers such a clear and detailed strategy to examine our lives in three-month increments.

Because I am a five on the Enneagram, I appreciate the clarity of the steps within the tool. This is a system in and of itself, and I love systems.

I tend to have an enormous amount of information in my head at all times, so the reset provides precise steps for me to take when examining my next 90 days. I was able to use this tool when going into the planning stages for my summer girl's Vision & Identity Camp.

> I was able to connect my REALIFE VIEW Document to every other aspect of the project in order to move forward. I am still looking at my 90 DAY Reset to align my projects, people, present, and technology components. What an invaluable tool!
>
> **—Gloria Howard-Smith, REALIFE Process Certified Facilitator**

What a powerful reminder that as we grow and become more authentic to who God has created us to be, that growth occurs, and then that pausing to notice that growth is part of the process. This is the power of learning to be present in our day-to-day lives. As we grow, our ordinary days really do become extraordinary!

“GETTING UP ON THE BALCONY OF YOUR LIFE ALLOWS THE BIG PICTURE TO COME INTO FOCUS.”

CHAPTER 10:
Practicing Living Full Circle

There is a poem written by Thomas Merton that I have read and reflected on often in the past 10 years. It has become so famous it is literally called the "Merton Prayer." I encourage you to look it up online and read through the entire poem. In this poem, Merton has several lines that speak such life into my soul. One line says, "I have no idea where I am going. I do not see the road ahead of me. I cannot know for certain where it will end."

Learning to do life differently has been a daily choice, and at many points along the way, I could not see the road ahead of me. However, I have awakened and become aware that, as Merton says later in the prayer, "But I believe that the desire to please you does in fact please you." Being awake, being present, is enough. Yes, it is enough. Nothing more is necessary except that desire.

No more striving for approval and living from doing, but trusting that, yes, I am on the right road. Holding both the extraordinary and the plan and ordinary of each and every day means that

I am now present to who I am "being" first, before "doing." I still pursue lots of things, but it comes from a different place—a truer, more authentic place that dwells deep within my soul.

As I sit to write this final chapter of the book, our daughter, Anneke, will be getting married in just six short days. Watching her walk down the aisle will bring closure to yet another season of life, but Dale and I are so full of joy about the amazing and wonderful man who will be by her side as she begins a new season of her own life.

They are a young couple starting on a journey of their own, and they have no idea what's ahead of them. Nor do I. I hold great faith that God knows and loves them more than I ever could. I remember God planting that thought in my heart one day when I was so sure that I could somehow control Eric and his recovery. In my quiet time, God said to me, "Teresa, I love Eric more than you do."

At first, I was taken aback by the thought that anyone could love my child more than I could and know what was best for them. Then I caught myself shedding tears over my thought that somehow I could out love God. The God who created my kids and brought our family together in such a special way.

That I somehow thought that I could have authority and control over anyone and their choices. What a pivotal moment that was for me and for my relationship with Eric going forward. I began to let go and let God love my children as only He can. Children are a gift from God no matter how they come into our lives or for how long they stay on this earth.

So once again the road shifts to a road I may know nothing about. What I am certain of is that I am choosing to live full circle in this season. It all belongs. Every bit of it. I am alive to my heart that is full of emotions, to my head that helps me reason the wisdom needed for the next steps ahead, and to my body that tells me so much if I choose to listen.

REALIFE in Real Life

When I first met Teresa, I was facing the cliff of early retirement because of a merger and a layoff. My whole life had been defined largely by my work. I had children, but I was always working full-time. When I went through the REALIFE Process and began to understand what a rule of life was all about, I was able to finally find a healthy rhythm to my life.

I learned how we establish the rules of life that help us define our priorities, our choices, and our responses in accordance with that rule of life.

It wasn't until I walked through the REALIFE Process with somebody that my awareness of self, deepened, giving me anchors that allowed my life to affix to something solid.

I'm now working with women who have come out of gangs and with kids who have come out of homelessness and abuse, and I'm helping them work through the rule of life to lead them into building a new life for themselves too.

I'm so grateful for the way Teresa put this program together to use a process and framework for organizing your life around important principles that form the anchor for a better present and future.

—Suzanne Handel, Private Coaching Client

Getting Real

When our son, Eric, was in treatment, the book *The Velveteen Rabbit* was shared with him on two different occasions by two completely different counselors, at two completely different treatment centers less than two years apart. God's ways are never a coincidence.

I remember going to visit Eric one night at a family visitation and him saying, as he threw his notebook and another book on the floor, "Mom, look what book my counselor gave me to read!" As I looked down, I could see the torn cover and the picture of the Velveteen Rabbit staring back at me.

I looked at Eric and said, "There must be something in that story that God wants you to remember." He shrugged his big shoulders and said, "Yep, probably so." You see, two years before this particular moment, Eric had been given this story for the very first time. I remember the counselor calling me and sharing that Eric had turned a corner and he had experienced a breakthrough. The counselor had really been struggling as he worked with Eric and was praying for something to bring to him at their next session.

The counselor shared with me that he wasn't even familiar with the story of the Velveteen Rabbit, but that in his prayer time before the session with Eric, it came to mind. He paused from his prayer and looked up the video on YouTube where Meryl Streep is reading the story. Later, during their session together, he showed the video to Eric and something in the story really spoke to Eric at the core of his being.

That day Eric and his counselor spent over three hours processing the breakthrough. It was a turning point in Eric's journey of recovery, but more importantly, in his journey of faith. It was at this point that Eric began to experience God in new and personal ways. Eric was an extremely smart young man and had all the head knowledge of God, but he had always held back from allowing God to really love him at his heart. Something in this children's story spoke to him that day, and for that, we are eternally grateful.

From that moment on, I truly believe that Eric's struggles became even more difficult for him as he began to truly fight the battle of what raged within him. The battle to be real!

It became even darker as he struggled to love himself and allow others to love him. As the wise Skin Horse says in this wonderful story, "But once you are Real you can't become unreal again. It's for always." Eric had become real, and it was a very, very difficult place to navigate.

When Eric passed away in 2017, we used the story of the Velveteen Rabbit at his funeral and the counselor came back to lead the service so we too could truly be real about Eric's struggles. We had no desire to hide the true story of Eric's battle with addiction. Our hope and prayer was that someone else would hear the story and begin the journey toward wholeness. That is our same hope even today.

The Velveteen Principles

The principles in this poignant children's fable are powerful and leave you with so many deep thoughts to ponder. Principles such as

1. **Outward appearance fades but inward wisdom is real.** "Because once you are Real you can't be ugly except to people who don't understand."
2. **Ordinary and extraordinary moments all belong.** "Generally by the time you are Real, most of your hair has been loved off, and your eyes drop out and you get loose in your joints and very shabby."
3. **Authenticity matters.** Showing up authentically with others in your life is important, but most important is being real and true with yourself. "Once you are Real you can't become unreal again. It lasts for always."

4. **Transformational love is often painful.** God shows us the greatest love of all through the agony of the cross. "'Does it hurt?' asked the Rabbit. 'Sometimes,' said the Skin Horse, for he was always truthful. 'When you are Real you don't mind being hurt.'"
5. **Your story matters. Connecting the dots of our story matters.** Remembering ourselves and pulling that story forward and into the present brings freedom. A new way of doing REALIFE going forward! Changed from the inside out! "'Why, he looks just like my old Bunny that was lost when I had scarlet fever!' But he never knew that it really was his own Bunny, come back to look at the child who had first helped him to be Real."

This children's story has so many principles to teach us. Simple principles but yet powerful reminders in helping to create this new *Modern Day Rule of Life*. Part of learning to live differently is learning to love ourselves as Christ loved us. I really appreciate how the Passion Translation of Matthew 22:37–39 says this when asked what is the greatest commandment:

"Jesus answered him, 'Love the Lord your God with every passion of your heart, with all the energy of your being, and with every thought that is within you.' This is the great and supreme commandment. And the second is like it in importance: 'You must love your friend in the same way you love yourself.'"

Eric struggled to love himself and to believe his worth was real up until the day he passed away. However, I know without a doubt that Eric knew the love of our Father in heaven, and that in his heart and mind, he desired nothing more than to live in that real and complete love that only the Father can bring.

REALIFE in Real Life

Becoming a REALIFE Process Certified Facilitator has been one of the best business decisions I have made. Being a facilitator is not only about having access to great tools and resources which bolster and complement my coaching practice but it's also about being part of a supportive community while on this wild and sometimes lonely ride called entrepreneurship.

Our community calls together have been the perfect combination of ongoing training and encouragement. I get to sharpen my skills in an environment where I'm being challenged to run the race God has marked out for me, while remaining true to the values He has instilled within me. The REALIFE Facilitator Network has given me the opportunity to keep learning and growing personally so I can serve and support my clients well.

—Tim Austin, REALIFE Process Certified Facilitators

Living Full Circle

When I resigned from working as a pastor full-time, I remember another local pastor asking me to meet him at our local coffee shop. As we sat at the table, he asked me why I was resigning. In other words, what is the "real scoop"? It was in that conversation that this fellow pastor gave me the greatest compliment without even knowing it. He said, "There is something different about you. You've changed."

At that moment, I knew I was right where God wanted me to be. I was living out my new rule of life, and it was showing up to others. My hair was no longer on fire and my life was looking different both internally and externally. A place of rest, not rush.

I had no idea of the path that lay ahead of me over the next five years. A path that would bring me to this moment of writing this book. The joys and the sorrows that have come along the way that are now a part of my life story. But I know that living differently is exactly where I needed to begin.

As you reflect on your own story, maybe you too want things to be different. Maybe you have had a life experience that has rocked you to your core. Maybe life has felt the same for a very long time and you know there is more, you're just not sure what the more is. You might not be quite sure what the next steps are and that's okay. I didn't either at the time and many of our community of facilitators at the REALIFE Process would say the same thing. But as Thomas Merton says in his poem, the fact that you have no idea where you are going and you can't see the road ahead of you, just might be exactly where you are supposed to be.

If that is you, I'd love to connect with you further and help you discern and discover your next steps.

Or maybe you are on the journey already, and you are a faith-focused entrepreneur, coach, or consultant and you would like to know more about our network of facilitators who use these tools in their business as they serve others. Then we invite you to go to www.therealifeprocess.com/getcertified and find out more.

One of my greatest joys is seeing others use these tools with those they are serving in their sphere of influence. As I turned 60, God continues to invite me to do life with others one soul at a time. It is my greatest joy to love my family, lead my team, and pour into the lives of our network facilitators as they multiply the vision of the REALIFE Process.

We all desire to live life from a place of rest and not rush, a place of presence not pressure, and a place that sees that every ordinary day has extraordinary moments, we just have to look for them.

Let me end this chapter with a prayer from the Iona Abby Worship Books that I use when I gather people together for our retreats, not unlike how we have gathered together here through this book. We indeed are now community together!

Creator of the world, eternal God,
We have come from many places for a little while.
Redeemer of humanity, God with us,
We have come with all our differences, seeking common ground.
Spirit of Unity, go-between God,
We have come on journeys of our own, to a place where journeys meet.
So here, in this shelter house, let us take time together.
For when paths cross and pilgrims gather, there is much to share and celebrate in your name,
Three-in-One God, Pattern of community.
Amen

Thank you for the time together through the words on these pages, for this I am grateful beyond measure.

~Teresa

“BECAUSE ONCE YOU ARE REAL YOU CAN’T BE UGLY EXCEPT TO PEOPLE WHO DON’T UNDERSTAND.”

—Margery Williams, *The Velveteen Rabbit*

ACKNOWLEDGMENTS

First of all, let me say thank you to each of you that have been a part of this journey as clients, podcast listeners, community members, facilitators, fellow coaches, and entrepreneurs. Thank you for your willingness to walk out this path with me and to travel your journey with you.

Thank you to Chris McCluskey and Mount Tabor Media for believing in this book and helping me bring it to life. Personally, I want to thank you, Chris, for seeing things in me that I haven't always seen in myself and for speaking them out loud for me to hear.

Thank you, Nick Pavlidis, for your continued support and encouragement to just write the book. Your process, knowledge, and wisdom have been a blessing.

Thank you, Victoria Mininger. Words cannot describe what your support has been for me during this book project. Your writing skills are amazing, but even more so your ability to walk with me each step of the way as a mentor, coach, and dear friend has made this book richer and deeper in so many ways.

Thank you, Catherine Turner, for your expert editing efforts. Your attention to detail helped put the finishing touches on this manuscript and ensure the book helps as many readers as possible.

Thank you, Dan Miller and the Eagleprenuer Mastermind. This circle of friends pours into my life weekly and raises the bar for me to stretch and grow and live out my dream of writing a book.

Thank you, Tracy Flori, my very first coach I ever hired, and those who have coached me along the way in so many areas of my life and my business: Brian Moran, Kim Avery, Dan Miller, Natalie Eckdahl, Shellie Warren, Carol Cox, Kent Julian, Cheryl Scanlan, Andrew Gorter, Jamie Slingerland, Rob Froehbrodt, Sara Anna Powers, Lane Booth, Justin Janowski, Mike Kim and Winston Faircloth. Each of you have walked with me along the way, helped to shape me personally, and poured into my life as a coach and as an entrepreneur.

Thank you to my Friday morning girls – Michele Vosberg and Deanna Gillingham – for your constant encouragement, inspiration, and ideas.

Thank you, Mark Ross, Chris Heinz, Tim and Eve Austin, Elizabeth Simmons, Carol Hassell, Sonja Wallenbeck, Cathy Yost, Phil and Lynn Brown, Angela Gage, Rob Henson, Janna Thomason, Tom and Rebecca Cook, Rachel Thompson, Michelle Mullins, Nancy Lopez, Greg Reed, Gloria Howard-Smith, Julie Loy, Susan Killeen Jones, Matt and Jocelyn Woodrum, Sharon Stenger, Natalie Guzman, Ann Morris, Georganne Goa-Chambers, Heidi Lewerenz, Tom Mabie, Rhonda Peterson, and Winston Faircloth. When you said yes to being a part of the REALIFE Process® Certified Facilitator Program and now the REALIFE Facilitator Network™, you opened up the world of what is possible when you follow a dream. Each of you have encouraged me and helped to shape this book by your input, engagement, and presence. But mostly by living your own *Modern Day Rules of Life*. I am beyond grateful to call each of you friends.

Thank you, Rory Noland, for being a light and mentor in my life during many very dark days. You opened my heart and my eyes to a new way of being in relationship with God at a time when I was searching for more. My soul is forever richer for having crossed paths with you.

Thank you, Clare and Scott Loughrige. Your guidance and direction as my Enneagram teachers have shaped my life and my work. Your friendship is one I hold in the highest value.

Thank you, Ruth Haley Barton and the Transforming Center in Chicago, Illinois. The years that I spent as a part of the community were some of the most formative years of my life and shaped so much of the development of the REALIFE Process® that is shared in this book.

Thank you, Sibyl Towner, my spiritual director for almost 10 years. You have held space for me as no one else could. You have been my guide, my mentor, my teacher, and my friend through some of the most painful and beautiful days of my life. God knew that I would need someone just like you to be with me and see me, and He sent you and your wonderful husband, Dick, to be a beautiful part of my story.

Thank you to my trusted circle, Erica Vinson and Terri Johnson. We have done so much life together that there are no words for what we have walked through. You are the ones who have stood beside me through it all and shaped this book. I love you and trust you not only as my dearest friends but also as team members at the REALIFE Process®. We have prayed for the day to come when we would all be working together, and those days are here! You have done each step of this process with me and helped to shape this book into the life-giving work that it is. Oh, the places we will go!

Thank you, Lindsay Sterchi, our newest member of the team. God has sent you at just the right time with amazing skills that make me look really good, but more importantly with an amazing deep presence that draws me into your wisdom and your wit. God has so much more for us to do together.

Thank you to my extended family. My mom and dad who shaped me at my core foundationally with my faith and values. Also my extended family on both sides. You have all been a part of the weaving of this story. Mom, thank you for encouraging me that I could write a book just like you.

Thank you to my family. Dale, Anneke, Justin, and Rachel. Your presence with me during the process of this book has been loving and kind. It's your story too in so many ways, not just mine, and I pray I have honored it well. What has come out of it will live on not only through this book but through the tool of the REAL-IFE Process®. From ashes comes beauty and now we are Real!

My Father God, thank you for allowing me to write my heart on these pages. This book is for your glory and honor and praise. My prayer is that it is a vine that grows and spreads exactly as it is intended.

RESOURCES AND CERTIFICATION

For a copy of the REALIFE Process® Workbook and other tools and resources , please visit **therealifeprocess.com/bookresources.**

To connect with our coaches visit **therealifeprocess.com.**

For more information about becoming certified in the REALIFE Process® and joining our REALIFE Facilitator Network™, go to **therealifeprocess.com/getcertified.**

REALIFE PROCESS® GLOSSARY OF TERMS

REALIFE Process® – A four-component framework to help you develop a unique, *Modern Day Rule of Life™* through REALSELF discovery, 90-day projects, time management, and spiritual practices for your REALIFE and sustainability in your REALWORK.

Modern Day Rule of Life™ – A rule of life is a commitment to live your life in a pattern of behaviors, rhythms, and routines. It is crafted through discernment, in partnership with God, as you consider the way God designed you and the values He has inscribed upon your heart. Once discovered and written, it serves as a tool and framework that can help you make decisions for your life and determine how best to order and align your days.

Component One - REALIFE Being™

REALIFE VIEW Document™ – A two-page document created to capture the balcony view of life, both the being and the doing, in written form. It is designed to be reviewed weekly as part of Component 4 in the Process. The REALIFE VIEW Document™ is a living document that is also reviewed and updated every 90 days as a part of the 90 DAY Reset™.

Needs – At the REALIFE Process® we believe God is the supplier of all our needs. Our needs are the basic things we require to thrive in our life and work. When our needs go unmet, we struggle to make progress on what matters most to us. These qualities express not simply what we want but what we need.

Values – Our values represent what we do and how we express ourselves. Values are how we uniquely live out what matters to us. Keep in mind that if our needs are not met first, we will struggle to live out our values.

REALIFE ENNEAGRAM Personality Profile™ – A psychological and spiritual system that gives us knowledge and understanding about our human behaviors and motivations. Some behavior patterns come from a very authentic place within us. These patterns can be our greatest strengths. Other behavior patterns have been adapted over time through motivations such as fear, shame, and anger.

REALIFE Process Mindmap™ – A diagram used to visually organize information that allows you to creatively brainstorm possibilities. The organic nature of the mindmap encourages free thinking in which a single concept is the hub and major ideas are directly connected to the central concept. The mindmap can be used in defining Areas of Focus, Action Steps for REALIFE Projects, and more.

Areas of Focus™ – 5–7 areas in our lives defined to provide tangible ways to live out a client's values. Area of Focus Statements are written in the present tense as if the action identified is already happening in the client's life.

Component Two - REALIFE Action™

Projects – 2–3 clearly defined 90-day projects that correspond to a client's Areas of Focus designed to move them forward personally or professionally.

Action Steps Pre-decided Actionable Steps with targeted completion dates to effectively move forward each Action Project.

Tasks – Everyday, ordinary responsibilities like emails, phone calls, errands, social media, and calendar management.

Component Three - REALIFE Time™

PRESENT Blocks™ – A daily block of time for self-care and soul-care. Schedule daily for 30–60 minutes. Schedule once a month for half a day. Schedule quarterly for a full day.

PEOPLE Blocks™ – 60–90 minute blocks of time for you to give your attention to valuable relationships. Schedule 3–5 blocks a week.

PROJECT Blocks™ – 60–120 minute blocks of time to do focused work on major Action Steps of your Projects. Schedule 2–4 blocks a week.

PREP Blocks™ – 30–60 minute time blocks set aside to buffer or create space for the everyday, ordinary Tasks and interruptions. Schedule 1–3 blocks a day.

Component Four - REALIFE Living™

Rest – Take an eight-hour break from screen time. Take time to notice. Practice being present. Spend time with those you love.

Spend time alone with God. Schedule weekly for 6–8 hours and every 90 days for 1–2 days during planning week. "Take life at two miles an hour."—Richard Rohr

Renew – Engage in something new—something relational and/or relaxing. Change environments and put the body in motion. Engage your brain differently. For example, hobbies, travel, day trips, etc. Schedule weekly for 3–6 hours a week and every 90 days for a half to full day during your planning week.

Review – A time set aside to review things that went well. Review Projects, review your calendar, record your thoughts and learnings, and reconnect with your REALIFE VIEW Document™. Schedule weekly for 30–45 minutes and every 90 days for a half to full day during your planning week.

90 DAY Reset™ – A day or week set aside to review your past 90 days and focus forward to recalibrate your REALIFE VIEW Document™, Projects, calendar, and rhythms of Rest & Renewal for the next 90 days.

ABOUT THE AUTHOR

Teresa McCloy is the creator and founder of the REALIFE Process®, a faith-focused company that helps entrepreneurs, coaches, and consultants develop and diversify their business by providing certification and training using the signature content of the REALIFE Process® as well as coaching and community to grow their impact and increase their income.

When she is not on the road speaking, coaching clients, recording her podcast, *The REALIFE Process Podcast*, or training new *REALIFE Process® Certified Facilitators*, Teresa enjoys being on the family farm, tending her wildflower garden where she loves to cut fresh flowers, enjoying a great cup of coffee with a friend, and of course, traveling as much as possible!

Teresa lives with her husband of 40 years, Dale, on their fourth-generation family grain farm in central Illinois. Teresa and Dale have two children: their son, Eric, who passed from this life in 2017 at the age of 30, and their daughter, Anneke, who with her husband, Justin, will be the fifth generation to farm the land.

Dale and Teresa have the smartest dog ever named Alley who really rules their home if the truth be told.

Certifications include:

- CPLC Credentialed Life & Leadership Coach – Professional Christian Coaching Institute – 2018
- ACC Credentialed Coach through the International Coaching Federation - 2019
- Certified Spiritual Director through Sustainable Faith – 2017
- Certified Enneagram Practitioner through ©iEnneagram Motions of the Soul – 2018
- Certified Speaking Your Brand® Coach – 2019

A free ebook edition is available with the purchase of this book.

To claim your free ebook edition:

1. Visit MorganJamesBOGO.com
2. Sign your name CLEARLY in the space
3. Complete the form and submit a photo of the entire copyright page
4. You or your friend can download the ebook to your preferred device

Morgan James BOGO™

A **FREE** ebook edition is available for you or a friend with the purchase of this print book.

CLEARLY SIGN YOUR NAME ABOVE

Instructions to claim your free ebook edition:

1. Visit MorganJamesBOGO.com
2. Sign your name CLEARLY in the space above
3. Complete the form and submit a photo of this entire page
4. You or your friend can download the ebook to your preferred device

Print & Digital Together Forever.

Snap a photo

Free ebook

Read anywhere

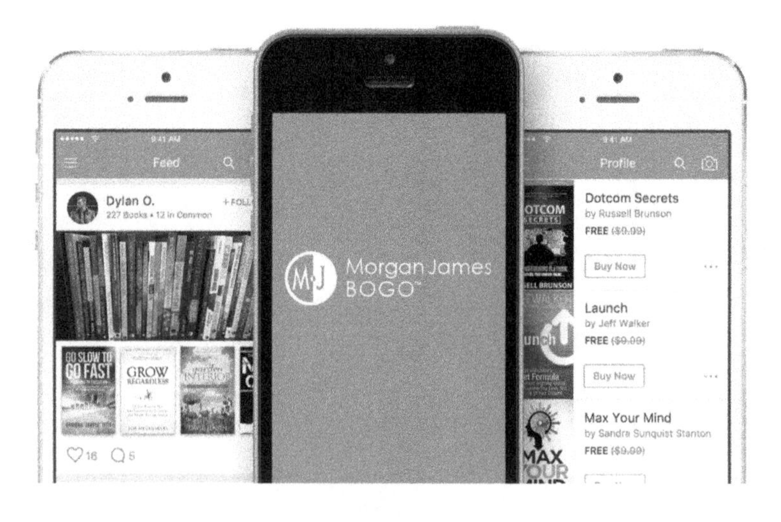

CPSIA information can be obtained
at www.ICGtesting.com
Printed in the USA
JSHW011526230922
30945JS00001B/14

9 781631 959066